The Crusades
in 100
OBJECTS

Per Anička,
apparuit iam beatitudo vestra.

The Crusades

in 100

OBJECTS

The Great Campaigns of the Medieval World

James Waterson

FRONTLINE
BOOKS

The Crusades in 100 Objects

This edition published in 2021 by Frontline Books,
An imprint of Pen & Sword Books Ltd,
Yorkshire - Philadelphia

ISBN 978 1 52679 530 4

Pen & Sword Books Limited incorporates the imprints of Atlas, Archaeology, Aviation, Discovery, Family History, Fiction, History, Maritime, Military, Military Classics, Politics, Select, Transport, True Crime, Air World, Frontline Publishing, Leo Cooper, Remember When, Seaforth Publishing, The Praetorian Press, Wharncliffe Local History, Wharncliffe Transport, Wharncliffe True Crime and White Owl.

PEN & SWORD BOOKS LTD
47 Church Street, Barnsley, South Yorkshire, S70 2AS, England
E-mail: enquiries@pen-and-sword.co.uk
Website: www.pen-and-sword.co.uk

Or

PEN AND SWORD BOOKS
1950 Lawrence Rd, Havertown, PA 19083, USA
E-mail: Uspen-and-sword@casematepublishers.com

For more information on our books, please visit
www.frontline-books.com, email info@frontline-books.com
or write to us at the above address.

Printed and bound in India by Replika Press Pvt. Ltd.

Typeset in 10/14pt Adobe Caslon by SJmagic DESIGN SERVICES, India.

Contents

Acknowledgements 10

Introduction: What does it all mean? 11

Emperors, Caliphs and Sultans 12
1. The Great Mosque of Cordoba, eighth to tenth century.................................... 12
2. Carved Ivory Oliphant of the Fatimid Caliphate. Sicily, eleventh century........... 14
3. Turkish Composite Bows, created by twentieth-century master craftsmen 15
4. The Mausoleum of Sultan Sanjar, Merv, Turkmenistan, eleventh century 18
5. The Murder of Nizam al-Mulk from a fourteenth-century illuminated manuscript
   of the *Jami al-Tawarikh*, the Compendium of Chronicles or World History of
   Rashid-al-Din Hamadani. Topkapi Palace Museum 20

Popes, Kings and Emperors 23
6. Hagia Sophia, and the Grave of Dandolo, Istanbul 23
7. The Temple Mount viewed from the Mount of Olives 25
8. The Kiss of Peace depicted in a relief sculpture in the tympanum of the church of
   Anzy-le-Duc, Saône-et-Loire, Burgundy. Probably eleventh century.................... 27
9. The Bayeux Tapestry showing Duke William mustering and leading a charge
   of his Knights, eleventh century... 28
10. William Marshal at a Joust unhorses Baldwin Guisnes, who survives the bout
    thanks to his chain-mail armour. From the *Historia Major* of Matthew Paris,
    c. thirteenth century... 31

A Youthful Venture 33
11. The Staronová Synagoga, Europe's Oldest Active Synagogue. Josefov, Prague.
    Completed c. 1270 33
12. Trajan's Column, Rome, showing Roman siege artillery, 113–117 35
13. Brass Pen Box showing scenes of Hunting and Falconry. Mamluk Period
    Syria, probably thirteenth century... 37
14. The Catapulting of Ibrahim into the Fire in Edessa. Page from an unidentified
    Ottoman manuscript c. 1600 39
15. Plaque from a Portable Altar Showing the Crucifixion and the piercing of Christ's
    Flank by Longinus' Lance. Germany, Lower Rhine Valley, eleventh century........... 41

La Gerusalemme Liberata 43
16. Jet and Ivory Chess Pieces from the Western Islamic World, ninth to eleventh century 43
17. The city of Maarat al-Numan's destroyed mosques following its uprising and
    subsequent bombardment by Syrian pro-government forces in late 2012................ 45
18. Pisa Cathedral and the *Camposanto*, eleventh century..................................... 48

19. Erminia tends to Tancredi's wounds, Alessando Turchi, c. 1630 50
20. Pilgrims at the Church of the Holy Sepulchre, Jerusalem, 2019 52

I Will Not Spare These Proud Egyptians 55
21. A Fatimid Armlet with Kufic script, probably Syrian, 909–1171 55
22. Astrolabes from Al-Andalus, 1050–1080 56
23. The Throne of Charlemagne. Palatine Chapel, Aachen. c. 790 58
24. A Berber Warrior of the late nineteenth century 60
25. Turkish Archers' Thumb Rings, Topkapi Saray Palace, fifteenth to sixteenth century 62

Securing the Kingdom of Heaven on Earth 65
26. Crak De Chevaliers, Syria, twelfth century 65
27. Karak Castle, Jordan, twelfth century 69
28. The Great Seal of the Grand Masters of the Knights Templar, showing the order's
symbol of two knights on one horse, c. 1158 71
29. The Walls of Malta, sixteenth century 72
30. Portrait of Alof de Wignacourt, the Grand Master of the Knights of Saint
John, Caravaggio. c. 1607 75

A Muted Response? 76
31. The *Minbar*. These examples are from the late medieval period 76
32. The Great Mosque of Damascus. c. 705 78
33. The Mantle of Roger II of Sicily, with Islamic Motifs, probably produced in
Cairo. c. 1133–1134 80
34. The Assassins' Creed Game and Media, twentieth to twenty-first century 81
35. The Arabian Horse. Timeless 83

Backyard Jihad and Détente 86
36. A Chalice carved from Rock Crystal. Fatimid workmanship with later
Parisian mounting, c. 1100 and 1225–1250 86
37. The Great Mosque of al-Nuri in Mosul before and after its destruction by
the Islamic State, late twelfth century and 2017 88
38. The Arsenal of Venice, twelfth to fifteenth century 89
39. A Reliquary Casket made from Fatimid rock crystal plaques, c. 1200 92
40. A Damascus Sword Maker. 'Whose swords were once considered the finest
in the world', c. 1900 94

The Martyr and the Saint King 96
41. Greek Fire in the Codex *Græcus Matritensis Ioannis Skyllitzes*, twelfth century 96
42. A Writing Case from the Jazira, with plaques showing the planets in character,
thirteenth century 97
43. The Ivory Cover of Queen Melisende of Jerusalem's Psalter, c. 1135 100
44. Counterweight Trebuchets, an invention of the early twelfth century 102
45. Camels carrying Projectile Weapons in Afghanistan, c. 1988 104

Of the Deaths of Great Armies and of Imaginary Realms 106

46. Coats of Arms, Cathedral of Saint Barbara, Kutná Hora, Czech Republic, fourteenth to nineteenth century 106

47. Details from Turkish Bows of the type that destroyed the armies of the Second Crusade, sixteenth-century examples 108

48. The Battle of Inab, by the fifteenth-century miniature painter, Jean Colombe 110

49. Prester John in a Few of his Many Manifestations, from the nineteenth to twentieth centuries 112

50. The *Douane*, *Dogana*, and Customs Post, an idea, for good or ill, taken from the *Diwan* of the Arabs to Europe and beyond during the Crusades 115

Monarchie Franque et Monarchie Musulman L'equilibre 118

51. Al-Azhar Mosque, Cairo. c. 970 118

52. The City of Alexandria 121

53. A Polo Game: an Illustration from the Divan of Mir 'Alishir Nava'I, Iran, sixteenth century 124

54. Yemen, Saladin's bolthole, should all his plans come to nothing 126

55. Saladin remains a potent icon for unity and resistance in the Arab world, despite the Sultan being a Kurd. This movie poster advertises *The Search for Saladin* 128

Fortune Makes a King 131

56. The Hakawati, a Traditional Syrian Teller of Arabic Stories and Reciter of Legends 131

57. The Assassin Castle of Maysaf in Syria, twelfth century 132

58. Devalued Dinars: Crusader and Arabic coinage of the twelfth century, Iraqi banknotes of the twenty-first century 135

59. The city of Jeddah. Its merchants' houses reflected the city's wealth and the fact that it was, and is, the gateway to Islam's holiest cities 137

60. Poster for the Movie *Saladin and the Crusaders*, 1963. Often seen as a celebration of Colonel Nasser of Egypt, who wished, and failed, to replicate the Sultan's deeds 139

Rose Petals in al-Quds. 141

61. A Reliquary holding a piece of the True Cross, twelfth century 141

62. A Statue of Saladin celebrating the Sultan's victory at the Horns of Hattin. Damascus, inaugurated in 1993 143

63. Naptha Grenades, a Greek invention, honed to perfection by the Muslims 145

64. The Massacre at Acre. From the Chronicle *Overseas Passages by the French against the Turks and other Saracens*, attributed to Jean Colombe, fifteenth century 149

65. The Chertsey Abbey floor tiles of the thirteenth century. Said to depict Richard the Lionheart and Saladin in Combat 150

Daggers, Détente and Deceit. 153

66. A Statue of Richard Couer De Lion from 1856, Houses of Parliament, London 153

67. Soap from Aleppo, a luxury enjoyed by Crusaders, and their ladies 154

68. The Two Tombs of Saladin in the Great Mosque of Damascus. The original twelfth-century wooden sarcophagus, and an early twentieth-century marble gift of dubious aesthetic value donated by Kaiser Wilhelm II 156

69. An Ayyubid-period incense burner with Christian iconography, a rare example of cultural exchange between the Crusader kingdoms and their Muslim adversaries 159

70. The Capella Palatina, Palermo, Sicily, twelfth century 160

New Jerusalems and New Enemies 163

71. The Four Horses of the Constantinople Hippodrome in their current home of the museum of the cathedral of San Marco, Venice, c. third century 163

72. The Basilica of Christ's Blood, Bruges, twelfth century 166

73. A Mamluk Bombard or Grenade, carrying remarkable engraving and artistry for what is essentially a bomb, thirteenth century 170

74. Modern-day Celebrations of Ponies and Bactrian Camels, the animals that helped to create the Mongol Empire 171

75. The Eleventh-Century Friday Mosque in Qazvin. Men, women and children were slaughtered in concentration camps that the Mongols set up outside Qazvin during their destruction of the Assassins Order. Even babes in their cradles were murdered 173

Islam Saves Europe, but at a Price 178

76. A Lustreware Plaque from an Iranian Ilkhanid *mihrab* c. 1300–1350. Vicious Mongol persecution of Islam had, by the turn of the century, been replaced by conversion................ 178

77. Mamluk Helmets, or possibly Ottoman copies made to revere the Dynasty that Defeated the Mongols 180

78. Banners of Mamluk Sultans, used to rally and to direct the best soldiers of the Middle Ages 182

79. The King of Jordan's Circassian Bodyguard. Distant blood brothers to the Mamluks of the Crusades era 184

80. Mamluk Emirs' Blazons on Buildings in Jerusalem, on Metalwork, on Cairo Window Grills and Textiles. Enduring signs of the dynasty's obsession with rank and power 185

Walls Come Tumbling Down 190

81. The Crown of Thorns, originally housed in Saint Chapelle, Saint Louis's purpose-built repository for the holy relic. Rescued from Notre Dame Cathedral during the blaze of 2019 190

82. Mamluk-Style Quivers, their wide mouths and large capacity enabled rapid delivery of vast volumes of arrows. 191

83. A Mamluk Mosque Lamp, decorated with the name of the patron who commissioned it, the emir Tankizbugha 193

84. A Mamluk Brass Bowl with Silver Inlay. The lotus, a motif brought from China by the Mamluks' deadliest enemies the Mongols, became almost ubiquitous in Islamic art after the thirteenth century 196

85. A Portal in Sultan al-Nasir's Mausoleum in Cairo. The arch was taken as booty from the Crusader church of Saint Jean in Acre by the Mamluks in 1291 198

Old Enemies, New Enemies..200

86. The Giostra in Arezzo, Italy. Twice a year, the knights of the Crusader Kingdom are remembered in a joust undertaken by competing quarters of the city against their old enemy, Il Saraceno 200
87. An Anatolian Carpet with Animal Designs, c. fourteenth century 204
88. Statues of John of Matha, Felix of Valois and Saint Ivan on Charles Bridge, Prague. The work honours the founders of the Trinitarians, an order that redeemed Christians in captivity under the Turks, and Saint Ivan, the patron saint of the Slavs, 1714.................205
89. The Chapel of the Holy Cross, Karlstejn, Czech Republic. Emperor Charles IV created the room to represent the New Jerusalem described in Revelation 21, c.1350 208
90. A Ceremonial Sword of the Order of the Dragon, a Catholic order created by Sigismund of Hungary in 1408. Its members swore to combat heretics and the Ottomans 210

The Slow Death of Chivalry..212

91. Fifteenth-century War Wagons were decidedly unheroic and stood against all notions of chivalry, but they afforded vital protection for infantry and hand gunners against cavalry and could also transport artillery shot and other tools of 'modern war'.........212
92. Tombstones of Heretics: Bogomils in Bosnia and Cathars in Carcassonne, thirteenth century..214
93. Eisenstein's 1938 film *Alexander Nevsky*, in which Teutonic Knights are equated with the contemporary Nazi state of Germany, and the invading German armies of 1914. The presence of coal-scuttle helmets on the Crusader infantry and swastikas on the mitres of the Catholic bishops drove home the message of colonial feudalism being defeated by Russian folk heroes 218
94. The Cathedral of Saint Mary of the See, Seville. Its bell tower 'La Giralda', is a minaret built by the Almohad caliph Abu Yaqub Yusuf in 1198 for his grand mosque, with later Christian additions 221
95. The Hussite Warlord Jan Žižka on Vítkov Hill in Prague. Planned in 1937, completed in 1950 224

A Long Shadow..227

96. Vast Mosques and Extensions to the Body of Hagia Sophia. Ottoman contributions to the greatest city of the medieval age..227
97. The Sacro Monte of Varallo, Italy. Started in 1491 and added to until the seventeenth century, so that those, 'who could not go on a pilgrimage might see Jerusalem'....................228
98. A Salt Cellar with Portuguese Soldiers and a Caravel. Carved from ivory in Benin c. 1600...238
99. Troops of the British Indian Empire. Cavalry on the Tigris and Infantry in Jerusalem, 1917. Their British commanders are also seen here mixing with fellow Italian and French officers to listen to a Franciscan monk preaching 240
100. Nazi Propaganda. Saint George draped in swastikas killing the dragon from a book about 'heraldry', and a Nazi Knight standing against the unholy faith of Bolshevism 244

Index..246

Acknowledgements

I have written my books across two decades, and across a vast geographical range. I have also met kindnesses and warmth beyond measure across so many lands. In the twenty-first century these benevolences have come chiefly from the hands and hearts of Nizar, Tarek, Jihad, Jane, Lisa, Larry, Natalie, Jeev, Ian, Vicky and Arek.

From back in the now seemingly long-distant twentieth century I wish to thank once again Dr David Morgan for introducing me, as an undergraduate, to the Crusaders, their doughty Turkish and Kurdish opponents and to the Mongols, and Dr Michael Brett for his engaging lectures on the Fatimids and the naval warfare of the period. I also wish to thank Dr Anna Contadini for creating in me, despite my fairly philistine inclinations, an appreciation of the miniature painting of the Mamluk period, and for helping me to understand how later additions to *objets d'art* were as much about changing the nature or intent of the piece as being simply aesthetic enhancements. Dr Brian Williams, formerly of the School of Oriental and African Studies, also deserves my gratitude for his encouraging responses after each of my books has been published.

One final thanks from the twenty-first century goes to Dr Anna Vičánková of Charles University, Prague, for her always charming, entertaining and cultured discussions with me on the topic of military castes in general, and on Mamluks, Crusaders, Samurai, Assassins and Landsknechts in particular. Her insights into the mythologising of the Samurai, another group like the Crusaders whose culture and period has been much romanticised and misinterpreted over time, have done much to shape this current work.

Introduction: What does it all mean?

This collection of objects means something, just as the Crusades mean something. That meaning has changed significantly over time, and has often been mythologised, and myths, to paraphrase Cocteau, often become accepted as history, and subsequently affect the ideas and actions of later ages. This cascade of ideals and 'lore' can be recaptured for us in the current age very effectively through a review of objects from the Crusades period (if such a thing can truly be said to have existed) and from subsequent periods. Some of the objects we will look at help us understand a little more the societies from which these ventures grew. They may also explain why the Europeans, once in closer contact with the East, were compelled by the discovery of its material wealth to take to the oceans and to explore further beyond the Near East and to seek the source of the luxurious items that were carried by the Italian maritime republics to Europe from Palestinian ports. I have also used objects from beyond the general timeline of the period to aid in illustration of material that is no longer available to us, or which represent ideas which remain with us today, and which evolved in the Crusades period.

That many of the patrons of these objects were men of the sword should not surprise us: the violent backdrop of Renaissance Italy and the simple thuggery of many of its lords did not restrain the production of exquisite works of art, and a passion for it among these often brutal individuals. Perhaps the art offered some redemption for the soul.

Many of these objects we will look at have changed their nature over time, as they passed through the hands of enemies and customers, whether that be through additions as in the case of the Fatimid rock crystal pieces to which filigree metalwork was added by French artisans, or deliberately unfinished Ayyubid and Mamluk metalwork that could be imported to Venice and there completed with local dynasties' heraldic devices. Objects also acquire new meanings over time. That a German Kaiser of the late nineteenth century should hold the tomb of a sultan in such reverence that he felt compelled to donate a sarcophagus to it would be surprising if it were not for the fact that the sultan, Saladin, had already been immortalised as the avatar of chivalry by Dante and Scott. Perhaps what we are seeing in some of these objects is a very constructive case of 'Orientalism'. What we see very little of in the period is an interest in the culture and technology of the West from the other direction, and that may offer a clue as to why whilst the Crusades essentially failed – the Holy Land remained in the hands of the Muslims – 'the West' won out in the long run. Though this 'closing down' of the Middle East to foreign ideas may well have had more to do with the traumas that Islam experienced from the East than from the knights of the West.

History is hopefully a search for the truth, or in the case of this work for the *meaning* of historical objects. Ranke gave all historians the task of *wie es eigentlich gewesen* – to show simply how it really was. But 'how it was' and 'how it is' must always be affected by perceptions, so alongside 'fact' I not uncommonly deploy poetry and romantic prose in these pages to more clearly delineate how meaning was mutated by contemporaries and by later writers. I make no apology for this despite the adage that truth is like poetry, and most people really hate poetry.

I firmly believe that we are still living with the consequences of the successful establishment of a Latin kingdom in Syria and Palestine in the eleventh century. In this work I hope to identify why that is the case, and why an understanding of why what happened then relates very much to what is occurring now in the world's central lands and beyond.

Emperors, Caliphs and Sultans

1 The Great Mosque of Cordoba, eighth to tenth century

Oh beautiful Cordoba! Is there desire within you? Is the heart that burns with desire due to your distance quenched? Will your famous nights have a return?

Oh my two friends, if I worry then the cause is evident if I can be patient it is because patience is in my nature if Fate bestows disaster then our today has wine and tomorrow is another matter . . .

Ibn Zaydūn, a poet of Al-Andalus.

The Islamic Caliphate of Al-Andalus in what is today southern and central Spain and Portugal had been a fact since the great Arab conquests of the eighth century. Indeed it was suggested by Edward Gibbon that had it not been for Charles Martel's wall of infantry and his defeat of the Arab forces over some seven days at Tours in 732 that:

The Arabian fleet might have sailed without a naval combat into the mouth of the Thames. Perhaps the interpretation of the Koran would now be taught in the schools of Oxford, and her pulpits might demonstrate to a circumcised people the sanctity and truth of the revelation of Mahomet.

This seems unlikely, but in Martel's resistance, and in the later conflict that has been given the perhaps misleading name of *Reconquista* led initially by knights of Navarre and Asturias, we can see the beginnings of several key elements of Crusading. The Franks, after their victory, began to believe that they were the people of God, the new Israelites, and whilst Europe remained very much hemmed in and assaulted from every side by Vikings, Magyars and by continued Muslim raids and invasions that went as far as taking the silver plate from Saint Peter's doors and enslaving boys and girls from the townships outside Rome's walls, there was a new confidence that grew from this and helped to create the Carolingian Empire.

Papal indulgences also began to be offered to knights to join the campaigns against Al-Andalus as early as 1063 and the notion of Spain itself being a sacred and holy land that was being polluted by non-believers developed quickly, with the Church of Santiago de Compostela and its treasured relic of the bones of Saint James becoming a focus for knights joining the endeavour.

Against this growing confidence and cohesion there was a worsening internal collapse in the state of Islamic Spain, a feature we will also see repeated during the early period of the Crusades in the Middle East. The Umayyad Dynasty fractured in 1031, leading to multiple polities or *taifa*. These states had neither the manpower nor the revenue to resist their Christian counterparts, and almost no inclination to seek mutual defence, and by the time that Pope Urban II made his appeal to the knights of Europe to free Jerusalem in November 1095 the Christian campaigns in Iberia were so successful that the papacy continued to grant indulgences for any knight fighting in Spain equal to those of the proposed army of pilgrims for Palestine.

Cordoba fell in 1236 to Ferdinand III of Castile, and the Great Mosque was rapidly consecrated as the city's cathedral with very few changes to its harmonious and astounding structure.

2 Carved Ivory Oliphant of the Fatimid Caliphate. Sicily, eleventh century

And only a few believed with him.
And they are few
And few of My servants are very thankful.
> Quran: Sura 11, Verse 49, Sura 38, Verse 24 and Sura 34, Verse 13.

The Shia Fatimid Caliphate had emerged in about the year 910 in North Africa among the Berber tribes. Its imams claimed descent from the Prophet Muhammad's daughter Fatima. By 915 they had added Sicily to their nascent empire and by 969 they had conquered Egypt. They founded Cairo, 'the victorious', and it was soon enough a centre of high culture and a producer of exquisite artwork in ivory, crystal and metal which was exported to Venice and Spain. Its universities and the great college mosque of al-Azhar were also manufacturing propaganda aimed at the Shiites of Iran and Iraq as the Fatimids began their assault on the Sunni Saljuq Sultanate and the Abbasid Caliphate of Baghdad.

The Fatimids obtained full control of Arabia and the Red Sea, and Syria fell to their forces in the 990s. In 996 the Caliph al-Hakim looked likely to complete the Shiite conquest of the entire Islamic world as his vast armies took Kufa and Mosul. Al-Hakim is infamous in the West for his destruction of the Church of the Holy Sepulchre in 1009, a crime against Christians that made its way into Pope Urban II's call for Holy War at Clermont in 1095, as well as his somewhat bizarre edicts requiring the deaths of all the dogs in Cairo, the forbidding of women to walk in the streets and the requirement for all Jews to wear bells and for Christians to wear large crucifixes of nearly half a metre in length at all times, but his death triggered a loss of drive for the caliphate and by the late 1020s economic crises and army mutinies had weakened the state to such an extent that in 1025 the black African troops of the Fatimid infantry were reduced to eating dogs just to survive.

A long defensive war ensued against the Sunni Saljuq Sultanate in the second half of the eleventh century for possession of Syria and Palestine and by 1092 the Fatimids held only the coastal cities, and only those by virtue of the Egyptian navy.

The long conflict left Syria nearly broken and plague and famine punished the region in repeated waves in this time, but worse was to come.

3   Turkish Composite Bows, created by twentieth-century master craftsmen

I am full of fatal arrows
My merchandise is pain and death
Learn by what thou have seen of me
I am the blight of this wide world

From an inscription on a Turkish Mamluk bow.

Saljuq armies were immense in size and made up almost entirely of horse archers. They were organised around a core of a well-disciplined *askari* or bodyguard but relied heavily on tribal warriors or Turcomen, who, whilst superb fighters, were hard to bring to heel and not uncommonly completely beyond the control of their commanders. Thus it was that as the Saljuqs pushed west to contest Syria and the Jazira with their rivals the Egyptian Fatimid Caliphate, the Byzantine Empire suffered a considerable amount of what we might today term 'collateral damage' to its Anatolian provinces from marauding Turcomen.

The Greek Emperor Romanus Diogenes was under political pressure in Constantinople to end the raids, and he was spoiling for a showdown with the Saljuqs. He brought his army into Anatolia in 1071 and he rushed into battle without really thinking about what he was doing. The armies met in a valley near Manzikert on 19 August or perhaps to Byzantine eyes they never met. As the Greeks advanced the Turks just fell away. Certainly there were Turkish archers riding up and down the flanks, showering the Byzantines with arrows and then fleeing, but there was no force to engage with.

The Byzantines kept coming on up the valley but still there was no real contact. Towards the end of this day of futile pursuit the emperor decided that he could not move any further from his camp and the army turned back to retrace its steps. At that moment, when the Byzantine army was stretched

out along the valley, in the process of changing their formation for the return journey and whilst the van had become separated from their rearguard, the Saljuqs attacked. The heavily-armoured Mamluk horse archers of the *askari* poured into the Byzantine column and broke it up and lightly-armed Turcomen rode down the Byzantines' flanks adding their arrows to the onslaught. Later Turkish manuscripts detail how a Saljuq trooper could loose three arrows from his bow within two heartbeats and these warriors commonly carried two quivers of arrows, one at their side and one across their back.

Many of the Greeks' mercenaries fled the field immediately, as did the Byzantine nobles who were the emperor's rearguard. The incredible impact and fury of the Turkish assault is testified to by the recollections of Michael Attaleiates, who fought with Romanus Diogenes on that day. 'It was like an earthquake: the shouting, the sweat, the swift rushes of fear and not least the hordes of Turks riding all around us . . .'

Looking back from nearly a thousand years later, the Turkish tactic appears very simple and it seems incredible that Romanus fell into the trap but the feigned retreat was a complex exercise, requiring that the enemy be engaged to a degree sufficient to tempt him on. It must also be noted that medieval armies were difficult to command and control in the field. Skills acquired in the grand hunts of the Turkic peoples were applied to the near annihilation of the Byzantine army.

The capture and subsequent ransoming of Romanus was enough to end his reign and the terrified Byzantines, fearing that the Turks would follow up their victory by crossing the Bosporus, sent missives to the pope asking for a Western army to come to their aid. Manzikert, and the almost unbridled panic the defeat induced in the Byzantines, started the chain of events that sent Urban II to the pulpit in

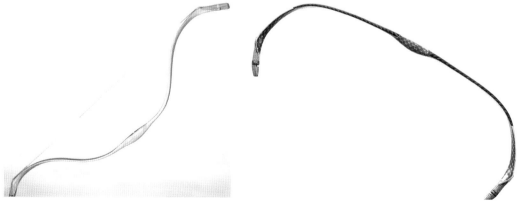

Clermont in 1095 to preach for the liberation of the Holy Land and the rescue of Byzantium, but it is evident from a review of the near-contemporary Islamic sources is that no connection was made between Manzikert and the coming of the First Crusade by the Muslims. In fact, the Saljuqs were not interested in the conquest of Constantinople. That would have to wait for another, much later, generation of Turks. The Saljuq forces turned south and began again their war with the Fatimids. By 1092 only the Syrian coastline remained in the hands of the Egyptian Caliphate.

4 The Mausoleum of Sultan Sanjar, Merv, Turkmenistan, eleventh century

God most High has appointed that to strike fear into men's hearts and as a token to renew that striking of fear again and again, so that a terror may be manifest in the hearts of men because of the desolation of the tomb and of the dark earth.
Discourse of Jalal ad-Din Muhammad Rumi, a thirteenth-century poet of Khurasan.

In 1097, as the armed pilgrims of the Crusade first breached its borders, the Turkish Saljuq Empire stretched from Anatolia in the west to the River Jaxartes in the east, in what is today Kyrgyzstan. It was also capable of bringing armies of immense size into the field. According to Ibn al-Qalanasi 400,000 Saljuq troopers took to the field to meet the Byzantine emperor in battle at Manzikert in 1071, and it

took an entire month to transport the sultan's army across the Oxus in 1072. Even in 1141, while the state was waning as a great power, Sultan Sanjar fielded an army of 100,000 cavalrymen against the Khitai in Central Asia.

As we will see later, the First Crusade never had to face even a fraction of the full power of the Saljuq Empire, and the story of the destruction of the dynasty lies entirely in the East. Sultan Sanjar was totally defeated by the Khitai on the Qatwan Steppe near Samarqand. He bravely rode into the Khitai lines at the head of his personal bodyguard of 300 men and emerged with only 15 remaining; a similar rate of attrition was applied to the rest of his army by the Khitai archers. It was to be only the first taste of the disasters that would come to Islam from Central Asia and which would eventually reach as far as the Levant.

Even after the Crusaders had descended into Syria and Palestine there was no effective response from the Saljuq sultans, and whilst this can, to a large extent, be explained by the fratricidal chaos that had descended upon the empire from 1092 until 1111, it must also be noted that Persia, Khurasan and the lands that reached towards China were always considered to be far more valuable to the Saljuqs than those that lay to the west of Baghdad. Furthermore, the threat from the East was always larger than anything the West could muster. The long-suffering Sultan Sanjar went to war with the

Ghuzz Turks in 1153 for these lands. His great cities of Marv and Nishapur were sacked and worse still, he was captured. The Ghuzz held him for three years in a cage, although oddly enough they still recognised him as their sultan and placed him on a throne during the day, and then returned him to his coop at night. He did eventually manage to escape his royal captivity, but died soon after, broken by his experiences.

5 The Murder of Nizam al-Mulk from a fourteenth-century illuminated manuscript of the *Jami al–Tawarikh*, the Compendium of Chronicles or World History of Rashid-al-Din Hamadani. Topkapi Palace Museum

Brothers when the time comes, with good fortune from both worlds as our companion, then by one single warrior on foot a king may be with terror, though he own more than a hundred-thousand horsemen.

From an Ismaili poem in praise of the Assassins.

The year 1092 saw the murder of Nizam al-Mulk, the chief minister of the Saljuq Empire and the author of 'The Book of Government', a precise manual of how to captain the ship of state, by the Ismaili Assassins, a radical movement of which we will hear much more of later in our story, and the death, amidst rumours of the caliph's involvement, of Sultan Malikshah. The sultan's wife, grandson and other senior politicians also all died soon after. The centripetal force of Nizam al-Mulk's government apparatus was lost and the Saljuq Empire splintered. This is was not surprising: the Saljuq Empire was, like so many other medieval enterprises, a family business, and the death of its head was enough in itself to cause immediate chaos. Turkish tradition worsened the situation, however, as each son was entitled to an equal share of the father's possessions, and so the state was broken up. Also, whilst these sons all had the same father, often each one had a different mother. Civil war based on a pushy mother's ambitions for her son may seem slightly absurd, but in the closing years of the eleventh century it was very much a fact in Iraq and Syria. Powerful emirs used their forces to their own advantage and formed unstable allegiances with candidates for the sultanate. In this poisonous atmosphere, regional leaders became deeply and mutually suspicious of each other and the unity of the state disappeared.

The Abbasid Caliph, al-Muqtadi, also died in 1094, but more important than this was the demise of Sultan Malikshah's brother, Tutush, the ruler of Damascus. When Tutush heard of Malikshah's death, he made a play for the entire Saljuq Empire. He mustered his army and, between 1092 and 1095, he conducted bloody campaigns against Aleppo and Antioch that brought Syria's already weakened economy and agriculture to near collapse. He then challenged his young nephew

Berkyaruq for the Saljuq throne in 1095. He failed in this larger enterprise: Berkyaruq marched out of Baghdad, and defeated his uncle at the Battle of Dashlu. Tutush was killed in the battle and Syria was left wrecked and rudderless, a vulnerable target for the Crusaders who were just on the point of leaving Europe's shores.

Western Persia and Iraq then became the main theatre for the contest between the sons of Malikshah. A civil war between Berkyaruq and his half-brother Muhammad continued until Berkyaruq's death in 1105, by which time the Crusaders had conquered Jerusalem and consolidated their position, without interference from the region's major power. Ibn al-Jawzi wrote that Sultan Berkyaruq, during one of his brief periods in control of Baghdad and before the fall of Jerusalem, had assembled a force to challenge the *Franj* in Syria but that, 'then this resoluteness fizzled out'. It is hard to contemplate how this expedition would have been funded, given the absolute exhaustion of the state treasury brought about by Baghdad having been occupied by different opposing armies some thirty times between 1099 and 1101, as well as by the constant 'buying off' of emirs during the civil wars. Indeed, al-Bundari described how, later in the conflict, Sultan Muhammad lacked funds even to provide for his emirs' daily beer allowance. Ibn al-Athir's verdict on the Saljuq sultans' isolation from Syrian affairs in this period seems entirely valid: 'the sultans did not agree amongst themselves and it was for this reason that the *Franj* were able to seize control of the country'.

Popes, Kings and Emperors

6 Hagia Sophia and the Grave of Dandolo, Istanbul

He was such a man in mind and body that wrath and love seemed to be bearing arms in him and waging war with each other. His mind was many-sided, versatile, and provident. His conversations were carefully worded, and his answers guarded. Being such a man, he was inferior to the emperor alone in fortune, in eloquence, and in the other natural gifts.

The Byzantine Princess Anna Comnena describing the Norman Crusader
Bohemond upon his arrival in Constantinople. From *The Alexiad*, Book 12.

The Hagia Sophia witnessed, in 1054, the excommunication of Humbert of Silva Candida, the papal envoy of Pope Leo IX, by the Patriarch Michael I Cerularius, thus beginning formally the start of

the Great Schism between the Eastern and Western Churches. In many western Christian eyes the duplicitous Greeks had been insulting western Christendom for far longer. The captivity, exile to Crimea and death of the seventh-century Pope Martin I at the orders of Emperor Constans II was still remembered.

What was fresher in the memory of the Greeks were the hammer blows that the Normans of Italy, Robert Guiscard and his son Bohemond, had been inflicting upon the Byzantine Empire from 1081 onwards. Alexius had eventually defeated the Normans' assaults at the cost of much treasure and blood and the general unpopularity of the Byzantines with the higher Norman magnates had required a papal political 'gloss' to be applied to any suggestion of aid to the Greek Empire. Urban's message of the suffering of all Christians under the Muslims, al-Hakim's destruction of the Church of the Holy Sepulchre, and the need to save Antioch and Jerusalem from the infidels may have been shaped to fulfil this.

The 'alliance' between the Crusaders and the Emperor Alexius would be strained from the outset. There is little doubt that most of the Crusaders were dazzled by the grandeur, majesty and riches of Constantinople. All of the major leaders took oaths of loyalty to the emperor; some more enthusiastically than others. And this was not surprising, certainly Byzantium had suffered many reverses since the irruption of Islam in the seventh century but it remained rich, powerful on the sea

and, perhaps, the only power capable of sustaining the Crusade on its long journey into harsh and dangerous lands.

That the relationship between the Crusaders and the states that they carved out in the East would be complex and not uncommonly antagonistic to Byzantine policy and interests was also obvious from the outset. The long-evolved diplomatic liaisons between Constantinople and every Muslim centre of power and trade ensured that. What the Byzantines had failed to appreciate was perhaps that their very wealth and dependence on the Crusade weapon would ultimately rebound on their empire and city. The church of Hagia Sophia also contains the grave of Dandolo, the Doge of Venice, of whom much more later.

7 The Temple Mount viewed from the Mount of Olives

Perchè la guerra omai non si rinnova, a liberar Gerusalemme oppressa?
Why is the war still not renewed, to free oppressed Jerusalem?

Count Godfrey to a Papal nuncio. Torquato Tasso, *La Gerusalemme Liberata*, 1575, Canto Primo Verse XII.

There were two Jerusalems.

Charlemagne had travelled there according to legend, and the Caliph Haroun al-Rashid had sent him the keys to the city. The sword he had carried at his side, *Joyeuse*, had hidden within its hilt the tip of Longinus' lance that had pierced Christ's flank. This was the holy and spiritual Jerusalem that lay high above the dross of this world.

This Jerusalem was fixed firmly in the minds of medieval Christians. Wibald, the Bishop of Eichstadt, did not complain over the seven years it took him to complete his pilgrimage to the holiest of cities.

There are five major versions of Urban II's sermon in which he called upon the warriors of Europe to save the Eastern Christians. The *Gesta Francorum* version does not mention Jerusalem but its writer was an anonymous Crusader of Bohemond of Taranto's army, and in the version of Robert of Rheims, who may very well have been present at Clermont, Urban called upon the memory of Charlemagne's destruction of the pagans and roused his audience to expel the Persians from the confines of Jerusalem and to 'let the holy sepulchre of the Lord our Saviour, which is possessed by unclean nations, especially incite you!'

Whether the kings, lords and common folks of the eleventh century should have listened to the clerics is a moot point. They did, as a contemporary and cynical rhyme made clear:

> *If you go to hear the preachers*
> *Do beware of clever teachers*
> *Who can with their style and gloss*
> *Make you a captive of the Cross*

Of the 'real' Jerusalem in the 1090s we can say this. The Fatimid Empire had recovered the city and its environs from the Saljuqs in 1098 amid the collapse of Saljuq power in Palestine and the *khutba* or Friday sermon was called in their name and in that of the Shia Muslim faith, but there was little time to fortify the city and its Turkish garrison had done little to make the city defendable during their

tenure. Indeed the Fatimids had practically walked into the city, as the Turks got generous terms for leaving. Palestine had become an unpleasant posting with a continuance of poor harvests.

Perhaps the departing Turks were doubly fortunate. For an enemy was now forming that had been inflamed by the Pope, according to Guibert of Nogent's recording, to expel the Antichrist from Jerusalem. For the enemy of Christ had now fixed 'his tents on the Mount of Olives; and it is certain, for the apostle teaches it, that he sits at Jerusalem in the Temple of the Lord, as though he is God . . .'.

8 The Kiss of Peace depicted in a relief sculpture in the tympanum of the church of Anzy-le-Duc, Saône-et-Loire, Burgundy. Probably eleventh century

You, girt about with the badge of knighthood, are arrogant with great pride; you rage against your brothers and cut each other in pieces. This is not the true soldiery of Christ!

From Pope Urban II's sermon at Clermont, from
the version of Baldric of Dol.

Western Europe, in the late eleventh century, was a dangerous place. A baby boom had occurred among the nobility, leaving a surplus of sons without lands who were quite prepared to undertake wars on their brothers for possession of small fiefs, and despite an upturn in the agrarian economy the lot of the average person remained miserable, as it was routinely shattered by internecine warfare.

There were impositions of truces on holy days by baronies, and preaching of an Augustinian deprecation of war for personal gain by the Church but the chaos continued. In 1063 the Bishop of Terouanne and Count Baldwin of Hainault issued edicts prohibiting unlawful war along with draconian penalties for breaking the truce: exile for 30 years, excommunication and denial of burial. It was not enough to forestall the endemic violence of the time.

The 'Kiss of Peace' was another attempt to ensure more orderly and unwarlike relations between the petty nobles but even this, though it lasts until today in the practice of many Christian communities, was not enough. In this little sculpture the embrace seems genuine but this was not commonly the case. 'He offers the kiss of peace, and then belches in your face,' as one writer had it.

The *expeditio* announced by Urban II and promulgated by a well-ordered clergy, the creation of Gregory VII, was a possible outlet for a society which was certainly growing in confidence but which was also tearing itself apart.

Progenitors of the ideal Crusader already existed in the form of the knights of the *Reconquista* and also in the 'swords for the faith', those knights and lords who fought for the pope against the Holy Roman Emperor in the Conflict of Investitures. During the eleventh century the papacy had been reliant upon Norman military power to maintain its cause but in the 1060s Gregory VII had reached out to all of knighthood. This involved the blessing of battle banners and weapons, and a call to dedicated service of the Church by *Milites Sancti Petri*, the 'Knights of St Peter'. The tale of the expulsion of the Antipope's forces from Rome by the crusading Prince Hugh of Vermandois, who fought under the banner of Saint Peter, is almost certainly apocryphal but shows how the French

nobility were ready to undertake a collective penitence and to follow the Pope as the leader of an army of the faithful.

Urban II called upon this body of warriors to take the Cross, with the promise of indulgences guaranteeing absolution of all sins to those who fulfilled their pledge, and beseeched them to ride 'under their Captain Christ to the rescue of Sion!'

9 The Bayeux Tapestry showing Duke William mustering and leading a charge of his Knights, eleventh century

Pro solo impetu nostro . . . By our one attack . . .

From a chronicle of the First Crusade describing how one Crusader charge was enough to break a Fatimid army apart.

By the time the First Crusade had taken Jerusalem the techniques of cavalry warfare depicted in the Bayeux Tapestry were decidedly old hat. The modern way to use a lance was no longer to hold it aloft and to stab at foes as you rode by them, or to hurl it pilum-like as a Roman legionary might. The full potential of 'shock combat' and employment of the full force of galloping knights and destriers came with the couched-lance technique.

The First Crusade was a revolution in delivery of the cavalry charge and not because its knights were better armoured or because their horses were larger and heavier than their Muslim opponents. By the time of the Battle of Antioch Fulcher of Chartres recorded that 'Our knights had been reduced to weak and helpless footmen' and what horses there were had been obtained from Edessa and were of Arab stock. The key was organisation. Creating an effective charge was, in the medieval age, extremely difficult. The charge is only effective if it is timed to strike the enemy at a point where his formation is already breaking up; charging against well-organised ranks, especially of mounted archers, was a recipe for disaster.

So much for timing, but what of delivery? The charge is a mass movement, requiring men moving as one – the shock is dissipated if members of the unit arrive piecemeal. The Normans, famous for their discipline and mobility, overcame this problem by withdrawing their knights slightly from the front line, usually behind their infantry, to line up before sallying forward. Even this manoeuvre was difficult if the knights were unused to fighting together. Of course, the knights of the First Crusade lived and fought together for an incredibly long period of time and the military genius of Bohemond of Taranto added further to the effectiveness of the manoeuvre.

Bohemond looked to fight on terrain that favoured the Franks and which reduced the opportunity for a mobile and dispersed battle to develop where mounted archery would be able to penetrate the Crusaders' ranks. A field narrowed by natural barriers such as rivers, lakes or mountain folds and slopes

limiting flanking options was ideal. His defeat of Prince Duqaq of Damascus at Antioch was achieved because he thwarted the Turks' attempts at encirclement by dividing the Crusader force into a forward and rearguard unit. The rearguard effectively plugged gaps around the forward unit, allowing the latter to organise its cavalry charge behind a screen of heavy infantry. Raymond of Aguilers described how all this took place on the day in question:

> Bohemond indeed followed at a distance with the rest and guarded the rear lines. For the Turks have this custom in fighting: even though they are fewer in number, they always strive to encircle their enemy. They attempted to do this in this battle also, but by the foresight of Bohemond the wiles of the enemy were prevented. When, however, the Turks, and the Arabs, coming against the Count of Flanders, saw that the affair was not to be conducted at a distance with arrows, but at close quarters with swords, they turned in flight. The count followed them for two miles, and in this space he saw the bodies of the killed lying like bundles of grain reaped in the fields.

10 William Marshal at a Joust unhorses Baldwin Guisnes, who survives the bout thanks to his chain-mail armour. From the *Historia Major* of Matthew Paris, c. thirteenth century

They became to Islam a source of reinforcement and an enormous army, and to the Caliphs a protection and a shelter and invulnerable armour, they were as the mail worn under a cloak . . .

Amr' ibn Bahr of Basra, known as al-Jahiz, 'the goggle eyed'.

writing in praise of Turkish Mamluks.

In Crusade histories one often finds the notion that the Turks were lightly armed and could be pushed from the field by the charge of mail-clad heavy knights, provided that the Crusaders survived the initial Turkish mounted-archery attack. This is true as far as the Turcomen were concerned, but in terms of an *askari* Mamluk it is far from correct. The *Gesta Francorum* tells us about these bodyguards that rode armoured horses, an unknown phenomenon in the West at this time. The problem for the Muslims was that, until relatively late in the Crusades, there simply weren't enough of these *askari* Mamluks.

Chain mail was the standard protection for both Crusaders and Muslim troops. Usama Ibn Munqidh, an Arab warrior prince of the twelfth century, relates how the double-link chain mail of one of his Frankish enemies allowed the knight to survive what appeared to have been an irresistible lance strike. It was not impenetrable, however. Albert of Aachen, writing of the destruction of the People's Crusade by the emir Kilij Arslan relates how the Crusaders, 'when they had seen the Turks, began to encourage one another in the name of the Lord. Then Walter Sansavoir fell, pierced by seven arrows which had penetrated his coat of mail.'

Both Crusaders and Muslim troopers were protected by a knee-length chain-mail shirt that extended up to the neck as a coif. The *hazagand*, a jerkin of leather and mail that was commonly worn

by Islamic troops in Syria. is definitely not light in terms of the protection it affords, but it is light in terms of the Syrian summer. It was taken up by the Crusaders of Outremer and spread to Europe as the *hauberk jaseran*.

The armour of the East never moved toward the total body coverage with plate that was a feature of the Western knight in the later medieval age as the technology and techniques of Islamic metalworking could create steel that was perfect for blades but it could not be formed into plates any larger than 25cm. Even in the Ottoman age Islamic troops therefore wore lamellar armour. It is this that has perhaps worked on historians' minds and created the myth of the heavy Western knight bearing down on unprotected Turkish bowmen.

Certainly the Crusaders had an advantage over the Turcomen once they were in close contact and it seems likely that the generally more heavily-armoured Franks were able to press their advantage once they were within spear and sword length of their adversaries. There was a growth in the number of heavily-armoured Mamluks in the armies of Saladin to meet this challenge, as well as the carrying of heavier axes and maces by Islamic warriors.

Technologically there was in fact near parity in weaponry and protection for the battlefield in the period of the First Crusade. What gave the Crusaders the advantage in the contest was something else; a fanatical drive and courage and a religious fervour that held them together in the direst of times.

A Youthful Venture

11 The Staronová Synagoga, Europe's Oldest Active Synagogue. Josefov, Prague. Completed c. 1270

Whoever goes on the journey to free the Church of God in Jerusalem out of devotion alone, and not for the gaining of glory or money, can substitute the journey for all penance and sin.

Pope Urban II's Privilege to the Pilgrims.

Describing the mass movement of people that took place during the First Crusade one chronicler stated pithily, 'the Scot gives up his fleas, the Norge his raw fish . . .' and given the fairly awful situation for the lower people of European society at the end of the eleventh century with corvée obligations to lords that tied families to unproductive land and the ravages of civil wars, perhaps migration to 'anywhere but here' might have been an attractive proposition.

Things would have seemed unlikely to improve, and indeed in 1120 Bernard of Clairvaux was still recording how serfs were inventoried along with other possessions such as villas and farms. France was also suffering at this time a spate of epidemics and bad harvests, whilst man-made cruelties came in the form of the 'judiciary', the *seigneurs justiciers*, who dealt out arbitrary baronial rulings over the peasantry but did nothing to control the anarchy wrought upon society by their vassal knights.

So, to paraphrase Hobbes, life was 'poor, nasty, brutish, and short' and added to this was the enticement of a *tabula rasa* as far as mortal sin went. A charismatic preacher such as Peter the Hermit, through promises that extended both to this world and the next, was soon enough able to gather a following so large that it has been conveniently titled 'the People's Crusade'. The moniker is, however,

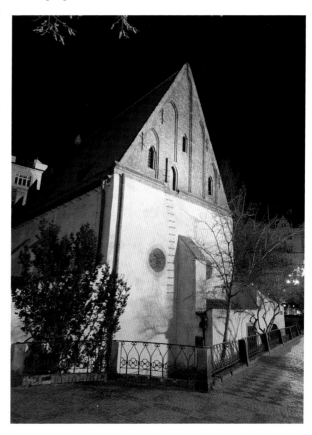

somewhat misleading. There was a considerable body of knights among the Hermit's followers and though he may have led up to 15,000 people across Europe and down through the Balkans to Constantinople, there was surprisingly little trouble from his followers.

The religious fervour that led to pogroms and slaughter of the Jewish communities in Cologne seems in fact to have started among the local Christians of the city, but the bloodlust spread quickly and was certainly encouraged by other preachers and leaders of spontaneous Crusading armies. The followers of Count Emicho continued the murder of Jews in Mainz and Prague.

That the Jews were equated as enemies of Christ along with the Muslims seems evident, even Albert of Aachen who gives us a second motive for the Crusaders' murders – simple greed – and who describes almost sympathetically how:

They killed the Jews, about seven hundred in number, who in vain resisted the force and attack of so many thousands. They killed the women, also and with their swords pierced tender children of whatever age and sex. The Jews, seeing that their Christian enemies were attacking them and their children, and that they were sparing no age, likewise fell upon one another, brother, children, wives, and sisters, and thus they perished at one another's hands . . .

closes his account with the conclusion that though the massacre was wrong, the Jews had indeed stood against Christ. He also seems to find the murderous sins of the Crusaders of Emicho to be only as detestable as those of another group who followed as pilgrims a goose and a goat that had apparently been inspired by the Holy Spirit.

12 Trajan's Column, Rome, showing Roman siege artillery, 113–117

Moreover, on the day of the Ascension of the Lord we began to attack the city on all sides, and to construct machines of wood, and wooden towers, with which we might be able to destroy towers on the walls. We attacked the city so bravely and so fiercely that we even undermined its wall . . .

The anonymous chronicler of the *Gesta Francorum*.

Siege warfare had not moved very far forward in over a millennium in Europe. The representations of Trajan's campaign in Dacia of a *tormentum* or ballista from Roman times equate pretty much with the machinery that the Crusaders applied to the first target of their campaign to free Jerusalem after being shipped across the Bosphorus by the Byzantine navy.

The problem was that fortifications *had* moved on. The city of Nicaea had walls of such thickness and height that the lightweight counterbeam siege engines that the Crusaders applied to its walls in limited numbers were quite incapable of knocking out even a few of its well-cemented stones, let alone creating a breach in a wall through which they could enter the city.

The Turkish defenders also employed their own artillery which included the 'Black Bullish', an immense crossbow that shot quarrels, huge bolts, and the sardonically-named 'Playful', a quick-firing mangonel, at any of the religious processions that the Crusaders dared to attempt around the city's walls. They also secured bales of hay to the walls to lessen the impact of the besiegers' missiles

and moved their own artillery to points where they expected the Crusaders rams and towers to be brought up.

This said, the Crusaders were tenacious and made it clear to the Turkish garrison that they would not move from the city until it capitulated. The *Gesta Francorum* gives us an account of Kilij Arslan's abortive attempt to relieve the city and to enter it via its middle gate:

> *This gate was besieged on that very day by the Count of Saint Gilles and the Bishop of Puy. The Count, approaching from another side, was protected by divine might, and with his most powerful army gloried in terrestrial strength. And so he found the Turks, coming against us here. Armed on all sides with the sign of the cross, he rushed upon them violently and overcame them. They turned in flight, and most of them were killed. They came back again, reinforced by others, joyful and exulting in assured outcome of battle, and bearing along with them the ropes with which to lead us bound to Khurasan. Coming gladly, moreover, they began to descend from the crest of the mountain a short distance. As many as descended remained there with their heads cut off at the hands of our men . . .*

The garrison wisely surrendered the city, not to the Crusaders, but on easy terms to the Byzantine forces accompanying the pilgrims on their march through Anatolia. Alexius' troops entered the city

quietly on boats via Lake Ascanius. The Crusaders watched the standards of the emperor being raised above the city, many of them in helpless fury. The issue of who was to be the legitimate overlord of the Crusade's conquests was first broached at Nicaea and would soon enough sour relations between many of the Crusader lords and their erstwhile ally.

13 Brass Pen Box showing scenes of Hunting and Falconry. Mamluk Period Syria, probably thirteenth century

Well could he hunt the dim wild deer
And ride a-hawking by river,
With grey goshawk on hand;
Therewith he was a good archer,
At wrestling was there none his peer
Where any ram did stand.

Geoffrey Chaucer, 'The Tale of Sir Thopas', *The Canterbury Tales*, 1387.

The Crusaders won through at the Battle of Dorylaeum in June 1098 largely thanks to the genius of Bohemond, who realised that the Crusaders' weak position – they were pinned down in a narrow pass of marshland and surrounded by Turkish troopers who continually rode by shooting arrows into the confused mass of infantry and knights – could be turned into a strength if the Crusaders used their infantry and tents to frustrate the Turks with a shield wall and a mass of guy-ropes whilst their cavalry under Godfrey of Bouillon, Raymond of Saint Gilles and the Bishop of Le Puy attacked the Turcomen of Kilij Arslan from the rear.

After the battle and as the Crusade headed towards Antioch Godfrey, later to be the first ruler of Crusader Jerusalem, was nearly killed by a bear whilst hunting near Antioch. The bear had pinned him as Godfrey had driven his sword clean through the flesh of its chest and it delivered a near-mortal blow to his leg. Muslim Turkish treatises and artworks of the period make it clear how a knight and a *faris* shared the same passions; hunting, hawking and riding.

The 'defenders' of the Holy Land and their protagonists the Crusader princes and knights have to be understood in context. As we have seen, knights in Europe were commonly seen as thuggish, predatory and violent by churchmen and peasantry in Europe. Equally, the Turks were commonly seen as oppressive, violent and loutish by the Muslim Arab population of the cities they controlled. The Syrian Arabs' disparaging view of the Turks is illustrated by the poet al-Basri's lines of the tenth century:

I am told: You spend too much time at home, and then I answer:
It is no longer fun to walk in the streets, for whom do I meet when looking around?
Monkeys on horseback.

The 'transformation' of knights into *Milites Sancti Petri*, sanctified and committed to the cause of liberating the Holy Land just before the First Crusade, had been evolving for some time before the

expeditio to Jerusalem. The later union of the 'men of the pen', Islam's religious intelligentsia, and the 'men of the sword' lay a little further in the future but would crystallize into the jihad and the ideal of the Muslim *shahid* or martyr and the *ghazi* such as Zangi, Nur al-Din, Saladin and Baybars that would drive the Crusader Kingdom into the sea.

The Catapulting of Ibrahim into the Fire in Edessa. Page from an unidentified Ottoman manuscript c. 1600

Let us now praise famous men, and our fathers that begat us.
The Lord hath wrought great glory by them through his great power from the beginning.
Such as did bear rule in their Kingdoms, men renowned for their power.

Ecclesiasticus 44:1–15

Baldwin of Boulogne's seizure of Edessa in February 1098 was significant in several ways. It was an important city, not just for its Biblical association with the prophet Abraham, but also for its economy based on the wool trade and its location. Armenia had long held a tenuous position in the region, squeezed as it was between Byzantium and the Muslim Empire on either side. The chaos of the Saljuq civil war had played hard on the Armenian cities of the region and when Baldwin and Tancred, Bohemond's nephew, broke away from the Crusade's main army with their followers they found themselves welcomed as protectors in Tarsus, Adana and other petty princedoms. Baldwin went one step further after being invited by Prince Toros of Edessa first to act as military muscle for the prince and to marry his daughter, and then to become his adopted son. It was not long before Toros was murdered, shot down with arrows by his own people while trying to climb down a rope to escape from the city, following a coup possibly instigated by his new son in-law.

Baldwin sent both horses and coin to the Crusade which was struggling beneath the walls of Antioch, and his largess to his brother Godfrey of Bouillon and the lands and cities he granted him within the County of Edessa were influential in the subsequent growth in Godfrey's following among the knights, and possibly his later election to the throne of Jerusalem.

It was also the first significant 'land grab' by a Crusader. It breached the oaths made to Alexius and also showed that many of the knights and lords such as Godfrey, Tancred and Bohemond, whose holdings were either tenuous or of poor value in Europe, would look to settle and rule in the East. Tancred would even go as far as to style himself as the Grand Emir Tancredi and to dress in silks and slippers.

The orientalisation of many of the Crusaders who stayed on in the Holy Land was, however, never so complete as to allow them to overcome the religious and racial intolerance that was inherent in the very nature of their venture, and there was never any large-scale unqualified embracing of the Crusade by local Christians. A letter sent to the Pope by the Crusaders shows the Franks' general attitude to non-Catholics; 'the heretics, Greeks, Armenians, Syrians and Jacobites we have not been able to overcome ...'

This inability to accept, and to integrate with, the local Christians would later leave the Crusaders in the same position as the Saljuq Turks were in 1098 – isolated and unpopular rulers with little local support to draw on when they were under pressure.

Plaque from a Portable Altar Showing the Crucifixion and the piercing of Christ's Flank by Longinus' Lance. Germany, Lower Rhine Valley, eleventh century

And when he had opened the fourth seal, I heard the voice of the fourth living creature, saying: Come, and see.

And behold a pale horse, and he that sat upon him, his name was Death, and hell followed him. And power was given to him over the four parts of the earth, to kill with sword, with famine, and with death, and with the beasts of the earth.

The Apocalypse of Saint John. 6: 7-8.

The Crusader siege and storming of Antioch, and the pilgrims' subsequent encirclement by a mighty foe culminating in a battle that quickly became the stuff of lore and legend, is perhaps the pivotal moment of the First Crusade. The Crusaders had already suffered mightily on their way through Anatolia and Syria through battles, the picking-off of stragglers by Turcomen raiders upon their column, and continuing privations brought on not only by the exhausted and distracted condition of the lands that the Saljuq civil war had left behind, but also by the scorched-earth tactics of their foes.

Antioch was all this and more. Peter Tudebode wrote that, 'the anxieties and hardships are more than I can recount'. The experience did, however bring an almost unbreakable cohesion to the pilgrim army. This cohesion was only maintained in the early period of the Latin State but it was central to its birth and the stolid defence of Outremer that the Crusaders put up in its early life.

The Crusader siege of the city commenced in October 1097, and it quickly became evident that the Turkish lord of the city, named Yaghi Siyan, was prepared for a long and unpleasant trial of strength. He quickly expelled many of the Christian men from the city in a fairly crafty manner. He first sent the Muslim men living in the city outside the city to dig trenches for his archers and the next day he sent the Christian men out alone to continue the task. Then, when they were ready to return home at the end of a day of digging, he closed the gates on them. They protested their loyalty but they were denied re-entry.

Antioch was Byzantium's child. Its walls had been created with all evidence of the Greeks' great skill in construction and its walls were over 5,000 paces long and were tripled in depth at some points. They were also two wagons' length in thickness. The city had six fortified gates and large parts of the walls could not be attacked directly as the River Orontes ran past extensive parts of the battlements.

A long battle of wills and of attrition began with the heads of Turks being fired over the walls of Antioch and the garrison responding with daily executions of Armenian Christians in the city's high turrets and by the spectacle of the city's patriarch being very frequently hung by his heels over the walls by the Turks.

The siege ground on until June 1098, and there was occasional good news to cheer the common people. Antioch's port of Saint Symeon fell to Byzantine vessels crewed by Englishmen. This relieved the army's biting famine for a brief period, and armies from both Damascus and Aleppo were defeated despite the shortage of horses.

The defenders ceased to believe that they would be saved, and the Crusaders began to believe that they could break them. The arrival of emissaries of the Caliph of Egypt to the Franks' camp in the late evening on the very day that the Crusaders had chased the army of Aleppo from the field added to the garrison Turks' belief that they were doomed. And then news came from Edessa that a vast army had been formed by Kerbogha the Emir of Mosul, and that it rode to destroy the pilgrim army under the black banners of the sixth pillar of Islam; jihad.

Terror gripped the Crusaders and even Raymond of Saint Gilles, who had hoped to rule Antioch in the Emperor Alexius' name rapidly submitted to the notion that Bohemond should become its prince after the Norman lord of Taranto told the princes' council how he could rapidly gain entry for the army of God into Saint Peter's city.

La Gerusalemme Liberata

16   Jet and Ivory Chess Pieces from the Western Islamic World, ninth to eleventh century

The Prophet said. 'The cases which will be decided first on the Day of Resurrection will be the cases of blood shedding.'

From the Hadith, The Book of Tenderness.

Kerbogha wasted three weeks trying to reduce Edessa, without success. The breathing space this gave the Crusaders was used by Bohemond to bring to fruition a long-planned betrayal of Antioch by a disgruntled and cuckolded Armenian armourer who now promised to deliver three towers of the city to Bohemond's Normans. By dawn 500 Crusaders were within the walls and the battle cry, '*Deus Lo Volt!*' was raised. The slaughter was immense and *à outrance*, or without quarter given. This, however, likely induced the troops of the citadel to refuse to surrender.

    Yaghi Siyan abandoned the city but this did not save him. His head was presented to Bohemond a few days later by an Armenian shepherd. Perhaps it cheered him, and possession of Antioch was certainly key to the Norman's wider plan of war with Alexius for possession of Asia Minor and

perhaps even the Byzantine Empire itself, but the Crusaders were now the besieged as Kerbogha's army arrived and the storehouses of Antioch were completely empty.

Desertions accelerated, despair set in and then a common man, Peter Bartholomew, told the princes of how Saint Andrew had appeared before him and told him that the Holy Lance that had pierced Christ's side would be found beneath the ground of the Church of Saint Peter. The Muslim writer Ibn al-Athir wrote cynically of the find:

> There was a holy man who had great influence over them, a man of low cunning who proclaimed that the Messiah had a lance buried in [Saint Peter's Church] in Antioch. 'And if you find it you will be victorious and if you fail you will surely die.' Before saying this he had buried a lance in a certain spot and concealed all trace of it. He exhorted them to fast and to repent for three days, and on the fourth day he led them all to the spot with their soldiers and workmen, who dug everywhere and found the lance as he had told them. Whereupon he cried. 'Rejoice! For victory is secure!'

Whatever the truth of the story of the lance, and there was healthy scepticism about it among the Normans and the papal legate Bishop Ademar, its discovery does seem to have restored confidence among the southern French in particular and among the common people. It was however Bohemond's tactics on the day of the Battle of Antioch that achieved the near-miraculous defeat of Kerbogha's army.

The story of Kerbogha playing chess the night before taking the field and the warnings his mother sent to him of how Bohemond and Tancred should be feared as they were the gods of the Franks and could eat 2,000 heifers and 4,000 hogs at one sitting were later inventions but his glaring error of allowing Bohemond to deploy his entire, and very slow-moving, infantry forces and nominal force of 700 mounted knights can only be excused on the pretence that he wished to ensure the destruction of the entire *Franj* field army.

It did not turn out that way. Bohemond arranged his knights in six lines and held direct command of the last of these squadrons, which gave him a strong spine to break the Turks and to avoid encirclement, but it was the infantry's fervent charge that broke Kerbogha's army apart. All the weaknesses of a confederate army led by an unpopular and haughty leader who prosecuted the battle with, as Herodotus would have it, 'that most dangerous tendency in war: a wish to kill but not to die in the process', were exposed very rapidly, and the Turks fled the field so rapidly that the most famous battle of the First Crusade may very well have been somewhat bloodless.

Fighters, as fleet as the wind, wearing white raiment and bearing white banners above them were also reportedly seen that day, as an army of dead Crusaders joined their still-living pilgrim brothers on the battlefield. Given such wonders it seemed impossible that Jerusalem would not fall to the army of God.

 ## 17 The city of Maarat al-Numan's destroyed mosques following its uprising and subsequent bombardment by Syrian pro-government forces in late 2012

I know not whether my native land be a grazing ground for wild beasts or yet my home . . .
A poet of the city of Maarrat al-Numan following
the Crusaders' destruction of the city.

Muslim resistance effectively collapsed following the Battle of Antioch and the Crusaders' route to Jerusalem was almost unimpeded. Only logistics, continued desertions and arguments between the Crusade's leaders delayed their advance on the city.

A Crusader force struck out towards Maarrat al-Numan. This ragtag army was nominally under the leadership of Raymond of Saint Gilles but in truth the common people and lower knights of the pilgrimage were pushing their leaders to action amid an outbreak of typhoid fever in Antioch that killed 1,500 newly-arrived troops and the important leader the Bishop of Le Puy.

What is more important about the attack on Maarrat, however, is what we see occurring on the Muslim side of the battle line. Whatever truly occurred at Maarrat – and we are given the choice between Fulcher of Chartres's starved Franks reluctantly turning to cannibalism or Ralph of Caen's children-devouring fanatics – Muslims from this point until the fall of Jerusalem seem to have genuinely feared the Franks and were reluctant to take them on. Fortified cities such as Homs and Tripoli appeased the Franks with fresh mounts and supplies. Of course, there was also a degree of realpolitik in all this. By aiding the Crusader march they effectively pushed them onto the Nahr al-Kalb, or Dog River, which marked the beginning of Fatimid lands.

Also at Maarrat the first Crusader assault was soundly defeated by a force of isolated Aleppan troops, and even when the Franks returned with vastly increased numbers, a hastily-recruited city militia threw beehives upon their attackers as they scaled the walls. Ibn al-Athir tells us how they held the Franks at bay for some two weeks:

> *The inhabitants valiantly defended their city. When the Franks realised the fierce determination and devotion of the defenders, they built a wooden tower as high as the city wall and fought from the top of it, but failed to do the Muslims any serious harm. One night a few Muslims were seized with panic and in their demoralised state thought that if they barricaded themselves into one of the town's largest buildings they would be in a better position to defend themselves, so they climbed down from the wall*

and abandoned the position they were defending. Others saw them and followed their example, leaving another stretch of wall undefended, and gradually as one group followed another, the whole wall was left unprotected and the Franks scaled it with ladders. Their appearance in the city terrified the Muslims, who shut themselves up in their houses. For three days the slaughter never stopped . . .

Up to a point, the townspeople had resisted the hardened soldiers of the Crusade, and a small group of Turkish soldiers had fought alongside Arab townsfolk and peasants. The Arabs of the Levant had not been militarily significant since they had been removed from the state salary roll by Caliph al-Mutasim in the ninth century. Whilst the Bedouin were wooed as allies by both Turks and Franks in the early twelfth century, the Arabs of the cities were viewed disparagingly by the Persian and Turkish professional soldiers of the region. These metropolitan Arabs formed the religious intelligentsia, or *ulama*, and provided the government with *qadis*, or religious judges. The most extensive military action they were involved in was no more than the organisation of the *shurta*, or local police. What would occur over the next few years, however, in terms of resistance to the Franks and a union between the Sunni *ulama* and Turkish military men, crystallised from the resistance at Maarrat.

The lower orders of the Crusade showed an equal passion for their task: they pulled down the walls of Maarat in order to force Raymond to continue to lead them on to Jerusalem.

18 Pisa Cathedral and the *Camposanto,* eleventh century

They that go down to the sea in ships, doing business in the great waters: These have seen the works of the Lord, and his wonders in the deep.

Psalms 106: 23–24.

The Crusaders were now in Fatimid territory and passed through numerous narrow valleys en route to Jerusalem in which they could have been halted by a small detachment of troops. The failure of the Fatimids to do so or to have a relief army moving to Jerusalem seems inexplicable, given that the *wazir*, al-Afdal, had received a letter from Emperor Alexius stating that the Crusade was no longer under Greek control and now had, as its exclusive goal, the capture of Jerusalem. The Fatimid garrison of Ramla, the last military post before Jerusalem, obviously knew what the Franks wanted; they abandoned their posts and fled. The Crusaders reached the walls of the Holy City on 7 June.

The Crusaders did not attempt to secure the coastal city of Jaffa before striking inland to Jerusalem, despite the fact that it was impossible to hold Jerusalem without access to, and succour from, the sea.

Perhaps strategy was simply abandoned in the absence of Bohemond, who had remained at Antioch, and the people's zeal for possession of the Holy Sepulchre.

Thirteen hundred knights and 12,000 men moved quickly to an all-out assault on Jerusalem. Both the north and south walls were assaulted as early as 13 June. The Crusaders, in their fervour, did not even concern themselves with building siege towers and engines, and their first unsuccessful attack on the walls was carried out with only one ladder. They regrouped and were heartened by news that a Genoese fleet of only six ships 'took' Jaffa on 17 June by simply entering the harbour there and watching the port's garrison flee. The cargo and crew of this fleet were brought to the camp and its Genoese captain was placed in charge of siege-engine production.

The Italian maritime republics did not only fight the Muslims, however. The struggles between Genoa, Pisa and Venice for dominance in the Eastern Mediterranean are a constant of the Crusades period and whilst there was certainly a degree of piety about their ventures in the Holy Land, as witnessed by the transfer of vast quantities of earth from Jerusalem's environs by the Pisans to the cloisters of their cathedral, an effective transplanting of the land upon which The Saviour's feet had trod, there were also hard commercial reasons for Genoa to send six armed fleets to Syria, and for Venice and Pisa to commit to the defence of Tyre, in exchange for, of course, warehouses, shares of taxes and customs duties and distinct colonies within the lands of Outremer.

19 Erminia tends to Tancredi's wounds, Alessandro Turchi, c. 1630

Multiply your supplications and prayers in the sight of God with joy and thanksgiving, since God has manifested His mercy in fulfilling by our hands what He had promised in ancient times.

From a letter of Godfrey of Bouillon, Raymond of
Saint Gilles, and Archbishop Daimbert to
Pope Paschal II, September 1099.

Tasso's poem *La Gerusalemme Liberata* has the charming Muslim girl Erminia abandoning her Muslim people to tend Tancred the Norman and to bind his wounds with lengths of her own hair. Nothing remotely so romantic occurred during the city's fall.

By the second week of July, the Crusaders were ready with towers and ballistas, and they had filled the city's moat. The Fatimid garrison had been busy too, maintaining an archery assault on any Crusader brave or thirsty enough to approach the one unpoisoned spring beyond the walls, as well as upon any religious processions the Franks dared to attempt around the city's walls.

On 14 July 1099 the attack began and Ibn al-Athir succinctly explains the mechanics of the city's fall:

> *They built two towers, one of which, near Zion, the Muslims burnt down, killing everyone inside of it. It had scarcely begun to burn before a messenger arrived to ask for help and to bring the news that the other side of the city had fallen. In fact Jerusalem was taken from the north . . .*

The Crusader assault on the city had been planned as a simultaneous attack on both the north and south walls, but Godfrey of Bouillon, leading the north wall's forces, had also outmanoeuvred the Fatimid defenders. Godfrey's tower had been swiftly dismantled during the night of 13 July and moved a kilometre down the walls from its original position. The Fatimids were unable to move enough artillery quickly enough to effectively repulse Godfrey's attack. That Godfrey's stratagem was a stroke of genius is evident from the fact that, two days later, the Fatimids were able to completely raze a tower that Raymond of Toulouse brought into action at the southern Zion Gate. Raymond of Aguilers tells us what it was like to stand in the path of this firestorm:

> *As the machines [of war] came close to the walls defenders rained down upon the Christians stones, arrows, flaming wood and straw and threw mallets of wood wrapped with ignited pitch, wax and sulphur, tow and rags on the machine. [This] kindled fires which held back those whom swords, high walls, and deep ditches had not disconcerted . . .*

The Fatimid artillerymen also managed to set fire to a vast battering ram, but it still destroyed the north-side curtain wall on 14 July. The next day they failed to torch Godfrey's tower, despite the use of a 'flamethrower' when the tower was within a sword's length of the inner wall – at this point the tower was too close for the wall-mounted mangonels to fire at it, and the piped and piston-driven fire-sprayer was the city's last artillery defence.

A section of the walls then went up in flames, as the Crusaders also employed fire as a weapon, and the northern wall's defenders panicked. Crusaders, under Godfrey's leadership, deployed from the tower and onto the walls. News of the breach caused a collapse of courage among the defenders of the southern wall too. Apart from a desultory resistance at the Temple Mount and the retiring of the Fatimid governor and his bodyguard to the Tower of David, from where they were able to negotiate their surrender and safe passage to the port of Ascalon, there was little else to interrupt the Crusaders' sack and slaughter.

Tancred undertook a small act of chivalry, well below the level that the *Tancredi* of Tasso might have achieved, when he guaranteed the lives of 'pagans', Jews and Muslims who had been pushed in desperation to seek sanctuary on the roof of the Dome of the Rock as Crusaders rode through the streets around the Temple Mount 'in blood up to their knees and bridle reins'. These unfortunates' lives were, however, taken by other knights beyond the Norman's control.

Jerusalem, like Antioch, now belonged to the Catholic world. Pope Urban II, the instigator of the *expeditio* would never have known of the triumph. He died on 29 July 1099, before word could reach him.

⑳ Pilgrims at the Church of the Holy Sepulchre, Jerusalem, 2019

Then our leaders in council decided that each one should offer alms with prayers, that the Lord might choose for Himself whom He wanted to reign over the others and rule the city. They also ordered all the Saracen dead to be cast outside because of the great stench, since the whole city was filled with their corpses; and so the living Saracens dragged the dead before the exits of the gates and arranged them in heaps, as if they were houses.

From the *Gesta Francorum.*

The Crusaders faced a dilemma. Jerusalem had been conquered under the banners of many secular lords and the one man who might have claimed authority over the venture as both a warrior and as a representative of God's church, Bishop Ademar of Le Puy, had died in Antioch.

Was Outremer to be a messianic community committed to the will of the Church or a 'traditional' kingdom under a lord or even king by right of conquest? Neither were satisfactory given that force of arms had delivered Jerusalem and armed men could be the only defence of this exposed island of Christendom in a hostile land, whilst no king could surely sit legitimately upon the throne that rightly belonged to the Lord Jesus Christ.

A compromise was in fact found within only eight days. The need for defence of the newly-won lands seems to have been uppermost in the minds of the lords as they elected Godfrey of Bouillon, who was undoubtedly a superb soldier, and who, as we have seen, was benefiting from his brother Baldwin's possession of Edessa as he could support more vassal knights and lords than any other contender for the

'throne'. The French jurist Beaumanoir succinctly describes how 'the lord is quite as much bound to be faithful to his man as the latter is bound in regard to the lord'. Godfrey had supported many desperate knights during the darkest hours of Antioch and the march to Jerusalem.

Godfrey was also undoubtedly pious and the initial resistance of the Latin Church's representatives in the city were perhaps partly overcome by his decision to be titled not as king but as *Advocatus Sancti Sepulchri*. The Church was also weak in leadership at this point as the Bishop of Orange had died before Jerusalem's capture and the Bishop of Matirano had been captured by the Turks after claiming Bethlehem as his diocese. Archbishop Daimbert of Pisa arrived only later, and notably tried to block the accession of Baldwin of Edessa to the throne after Godfrey's death.

The established 'practice' of feudal law may also have decided the matter in favour of the secular rather than the spiritual lords of the new territory. Having a 'ready-made' government apparatus, however flawed, would have been an important factor in the creation of a rapid and effective administration and defence of Outremer, just as it had been in the Norman conquest of England. Raymond of Aguilers describes how much of the horse-trading and negotiations between the lords centred on who 'should collect the tribute of the regions, to whom the peasants of the land could turn, and who would see to it that the land was not further devastated'.

Devastation was potentially at hand. Egypt had finally been stirred to stern action, and had dispatched an army against the nascent Crusader state. There was a rapid election of Arnulf, the chaplain of Robert of Normandy (a supporter of Godfrey in the elections for ruler), as Patriarch of the city. His 'incontinence' during the pilgrimage and the fact that he had never held a significant office in the Church led to much mutterings from the higher clergy and the singing of many a ribald song about the new spiritual leader of the celestial city. What swung the election in his favour was his discovery of fragments of the True Cross that had been hidden away by a Syrian Christian monk and which were then reshaped through many days of industry into a miniscule imitation of the instrument of Christ's death. This act guaranteed his acceptance by the laity.

The tiny artefact was further enriched with silver and gold and carried through the streets into the Holy Sepulchre. Muslims had commonly mocked Christians as being *Abd al-Salib*, Slaves of the Cross, but as we will see, a Crusader army with the Cross as its vanguard was capable of deeds far beyond its numbers.

I Will Not Spare These Proud Egyptians

21 A Fatimid Armlet with Kufic script, probably Syrian, 909–1171

> *I will not spare these proud Egyptians,*
> *Nor change my martial observations*
> *For all the wealth of Gihon's golden waves,*
> *Or for the love of Venus, would she leave*
> *The angry god of arms and lie with me.*
>
> Christopher Marlowe, *Tamburlaine the Great*, Part I, Act V, Scene I.

Egypt's tardy response to the Crusade's march on Palestine was too late to save Jerusalem. It was also discovered easily, when the Crusaders captured scouts on the coast north of Ascalon where the army was gathering. Godfrey took the initiative and marched on the Fatimid port. The Egyptian army should have been more than adequate to defeat the Crusaders. It met them in open country and outnumbered them two to one. It was poor generalship, and some lack of fortune, that ultimately brought failure.

The Egyptian army was ethnically mixed. Fulcher of Chartres described Ethiopians in the Jerusalem garrison, and the Fatimid infantry were commonly Sudanese. A wing of Arab cavalry was usually

deployed alongside heavier Turkish cavalry. Each unit had clearly defined tactical roles. The Fatimid army had been reduced from the 100,000 men of the 1060s, due to Egypt's shrinking fortunes, but the army of the early twelfth century was in fact better for this downsizing. It was more professional and less tribally split, and was well provisioned, at least initially. A treatise by al-Tarsusi, though it was written for Saladin, shows how the Fatimid army was divided down by into distinct roles:

> *Place the infantry ahead of the cavalry to make a firm fortress. In front of every foot soldier place a kite-shaped shield or a screen as a protection against those who attack with sword, spear, or arrow. Behind each pair of men place an archer with a crossbow or with heavy bows and arrows. Their role is to drive back the attackers. The cavalry and heavy defensive cavalry to the rear are separated from danger by the archers. Meanwhile the offensive cavalry wait to deliver a charge. Troops are grouped together into units with a prearranged separation between them. When the cavalry return from their charge, and flow back towards their point of departure, the infantry return to their original places, reassembling like the elements of a building. On the field of battle it is necessary to arrange the ranks gathered into squadrons of soldiers and with the cavalry grouped flag by flag and battalion by battalion. This should be done when it is the enemy's habit to charge in a mass and to rely for impact on separate detachments of their force, as is the case with the evil Frank Crusaders.*

This all sounds highly effective in theory but battle is always a chancy business and there are no guarantees that the enemy will play his part in one's strategy. It is difficult to reconstruct the Battle of Ascalon from the sources, but the evidence available indicates that the Fatimid force was stationary and presented the perfect target – a fixed mass of men – for the Crusader charge, which rapidly turned their 'fortress' of troops into a chaotic shambles of panicking men. One charge was enough, and it seems that the Fatimids were caught out by the speed of the Crusaders' move to the charge. After so long fighting together, the Crusader knights would have been able to organise very swiftly behind an equally quickly formed wall of infantry. The Fatimid deployment would have taken far longer to organise. The *wazir*, Al-Afdal, had also failed to set scouts and the Crusaders' pre-dawn attack caught him unawares.

The Fatimid army had been badly mauled. As a result of these losses and the fact that so many of the Fatimid troops were slaughtered in their pell-mell retreat to Ascalon, it was two years before the *wazir* would return with his army to attempt once more to push the Crusaders from Palestine.

Astrolabes from Al-Andalus, 1050–1080

> *It is preferable to hear the flatulence of camels, than the prayers of fishes.*
>
> Medieval Arab Proverb.

The Muslims had been the main players in the Mediterranean from the eighth to the eleventh century but new shipbuilding technologies were developed by the Italian maritime republics in the early twelfth century. A ship could be produced as a frame of ribs and spars, which was far faster than the laborious planking method that Egyptian ships continued to be built by. The deteriorating economy

of Egypt, as well as a lack of raw materials, also precluded any chance of the Fatimids winning a naval arms race against the Pisans, Genoese and Venetians.

It also appears that, during this period, the Italians were better sailors than the Muslims. The Fatimids never developed a separate ministry for the upkeep of the fleet and, perhaps more importantly, for training captains. The fleet came under the *diwan al-jihad*, or department of war, and it was only much later when Saladin came to power in Egypt that a *diwan al-ustal*, or department of the navy, was created. Without an active admiralty, the navy lacked leadership and any esprit de corps. Contemporary Muslim writers consistently excuse the navy's tardy arrival at the scene of fallen Muslim cities, but there is a detectable undercurrent in the chronicles that the Fatimid navy was lacking in courage. Low morale, low pay and the fact that rowers for the galleys were press-ganged and not volunteers were all likely causes. Generally the Fatimid navy would not sail in winter, unlike the Italians, and nature itself seemed to be against the Egyptians – the Mediterranean has a strong current that runs from west to east, along the African shore, which, along with prevailing winds largely from the north, made its eastern shores a constant danger to vessels of this period, none of which could tack into the wind. Under oar-power these ships could only make an average speed of about two knots (two nautical miles per hour) and the large crew of every galley had to be fed and supplied with water. No galleys of this period could stay at sea long enough or had sufficient offshore range to effectively patrol the open sea or effect a true naval blockade and thereby claim 'ownership' over the Eastern Mediterranean.

The loss of Cyprus and Crete to the Byzantines, and of Sicily to the Normans, before the First Crusade was launched severely restricted the ability of the Egyptian fleet to protect the Syrian coast but the Fatimids still maintained a concerted if onerous campaign to bring succour to their Syrian coastal cities until 1124.

The Genoese took Jaffa in 1103, and the Fatimid fleet harboured there scattered along the coast and brought relief to the besieged cities of Tyre and Acre. The beaching on the Palestinian coast of 25 ships in a storm and the capture of their 2,000 oarsmen in 1105 was a heavy blow to the navy, but it enjoyed success at Sidon in August 1108 against Baldwin's attempts to take the city. The fleet was, however, trapped in Beirut's harbour and badly mauled during the city's fall in April 1110; it also failed to sail to Sidon's rescue in December 1110.

As each of these Syrian ports fell to the Crusaders the Italian Republics' stranglehold on the Eastern Mediterranean increased.

23 The Throne of Charlemagne. Palatine Chapel, Aachen, c. 790

King of the Latin People of Jerusalem, King of Babylon and Asia, Commanders of the Christian Army of Asia . . .

A selection of the many titles experimented with by the new Latin rulers of the Holy Land.

Godfrey died on 18 July 1100. All the Muslim sources claim that Godfrey was killed by a Muslim arrow whilst besieging Acre. Western sources state that he died of an illness in Caesarea.

The succession of his brother Baldwin of Edessa was 'natural' in terms of consanguinity but contestable simply because the throne he would sit upon was the holiest in Christendom and had been obtained through the efforts of multiple lords, the Church and the laity.

Bohemond of Antioch was certainly the preferred candidate of Archbishop Daimbert of Pisa, who had recently arrived as the new Patriarch of Jerusalem. He certainly favoured the Normans of Outremer and was suspicious of Baldwin given his family's pro-imperial history during the conflict between the papacy and the Holy Roman Emperor over investitures.

Even Baldwin's journey from Edessa to Jerusalem was made perilous by attempted ambushes by Turks, very possibly acting on intelligence given to them by the Normans. In fact Baldwin was fortunate that Bohemond had been captured by the Turkish lord Danishmend of western Anatolia and Tancred was away from the Holy City with Daimbert besieging Haifa when he arrived at Jerusalem.

Baldwin acted quickly after he arrived on 9 November. He assumed the title of king on 13 November and was crowned in the Church of the Nativity in Bethlehem on Christmas Day, just as Charlemagne had been in Rome in the year 800. Legend told of Charlemagne's crowning in Jerusalem and this 'lore' had transferred into the creation of the Jerusalem throne in Aachen. That Baldwin identified with the 'wonder working king' is not surprising, and he used such ideas to ensure that the King of Jerusalem would not be the vassal of the Church. Through his influence the men who held the throne of Jerusalem would became far more powerful than Godfrey had ever been. The prestige attached to possession of the holiest throne in Christendom partly accounted for this, and the king also held the most lands, which could be distributed as fiefs and could also use finance-based fiefs from the trade of the kingdom to maintain his base of vassals.

From Baldwin onwards the king also selected the Patriarch of Jerusalem and he appears to have been able, generally, to avoid the Church acting as an alternative power in the state, though Baldwin II continually disputed the exercise of power in the Kingdom with the Patriarch.

The strength of the King of Jerusalem and his executive power in the other Latin states in the first half of the twelfth century despite the existence of four distinct states – Edessa, Tripoli, Antioch and Jerusalem – is shown by Baldwin II's campaigns for Tripoli and his holding of the regency of Antioch 'in trust' for Bohemond II between 1119 and 1126. His status in the principality of Antioch and Counties of Edessa and Tripoli appears to have been similar to that of contemporary European monarchs, in that he could not directly exert his power as a king but was *primus inter pares*.

The opportunities afforded the Crusaders by an ineffective and disunited Muslim response to their incursions were more than ample for these courageous, highly motivated and effective fighters to build a strong state that would be difficult for their later foes to eradicate.

 # A Berber Warrior of the late nineteenth century

Verily, a Berber had entered into our presence even though we all hold him in contempt and despise his people . . .

The *Ansari* or Helpers of the Prophet Muhammad in conversation with Muhammad's mother, Aisha. From an unlikely Prophetic Hadith originating in medieval North Africa.

The Fatimids reopened the war with the Crusaders again in July 1101 by attempting to take Ramla and thereby to cut off Jerusalem from Jaffa. The Crusader force which met them was small, with only 260 knights divided into six squadrons, which were dispatched from behind a curtain of infantry into the Fatimid army as paired units. The Fatimid centre held and Fulcher of Chartres tells us that Baldwin had to ride with his last squadron into the massed ranks of the Muslims in order to break them. The wings broke with the shock of this last charge, but the Fatimids held in the centre and came close to winning the battle through simple attrition. However, their emir was killed and the army's resistance then collapsed. The main army was also failed by indiscipline from its Berber cavalry, which had ridden out wide during the early Crusader charges and had surprised their infantry line. They rode down the infantry but then left the battle and rode on to Jaffa in search of loot. Their desertion allowed Baldwin to launch his last charge without fear of encirclement, despite the loss of his supporting infantry.

It is possible of course that the Berbers just didn't feel capable of taking on the Crusader knights. They did not have the deadly archery fusillade of the Turcomen to rely on and they were not heavily armoured like the *askari* Mamluks. They carried a lance and sword only, and it is notable that the Muslims' lances lengthened over the period of the Crusades, as if every soldier was reluctant to get within reach of the knights' battle swords. The Berber cavalry's reluctance to continue the fight was also symptomatic of the deep-rooted problems of Fatimid leadership and finance: Egypt had not fully recovered from the famine that had affected it from 1066 to 1073, and the revenues of Syria had now,

of course, also been lost. Low army morale and internecine arguments among its commanders over allocation of lands and revenues were common.

The Fatimids took on the Crusaders again in May 1102 at Ramla under al-Afdal's son, Sharaf. They defeated Baldwin's small force but they were unable to dispatch enough of his army to make the victory immediately valuable. They also failed to take Jaffa, which made their victory a very hollow one. Once again, Baldwin had charged at the centre of the Fatimid force, but this time it had held firm and the Crusader charge shattered. Baldwin fled from the field and hid in a reed bed. He was badly burnt when the reeds were set on fire by his pursuers, but escaped to Arsuf. Sharaf was unlucky not to take Jaffa, where the Latin infantry set up a fierce defence. A Frankish fleet smashed through the Fatimid naval blockade of the city and a bloody battle then broke out between the Fatimid army and its own fleet's marines. The Egyptians carried out a wholesale slaughter of the survivors of the Battle of Ramla, but when Baldwin led fresh forces out from Jaffa and engaged Sharaf once more the Fatimid troops broke under his charge and fled the field.

25 Turkish Archers' Thumb Rings, Topkapi Saray Palace, fifteenth to sixteenth century

Anything in which a man passes his time is vain except for shooting with his bow, training his horse, or dallying with his wife. These three things are right. He who abandons archery after having learnt it is ungrateful to the one who taught him.

Attributed to the Prophet Muhammad.

The Turkish bow was drawn to the ear rather than to the eye in order to maximise its power and the bowstring was taken up with the thumb as the pull required, some 30kg, was too much for a finger pull. Thumb rings, used to prevent the string cutting the thumb, were made of bone, stone or jade, and became increasingly elaborate. The later Ottoman sultans were never to be seen without an ornate thumb ring. With this long pull the Turkish composite bow had an effective range of about 200m but at this distance it could not kill an armoured man.

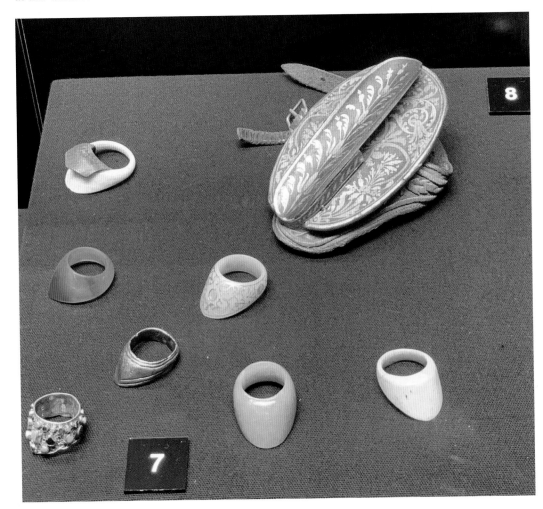

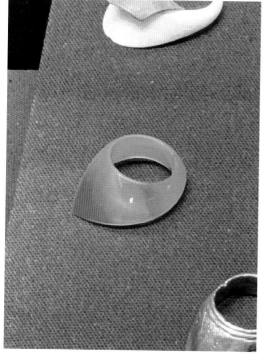

The weapon became deadly, even to troops wearing mail, at 75m, and in the summer of 1101 the troopers of Kilij Arslan used it to almost totally destroy a series of vast Crusader armies that attempted to cross Anatolia. The first contact was near a small village named Merzifun. It had taken several days of hit-and-run raids on the column and the poisoning of wells to steer the Crusaders to the killing field. The battle then developed over several days. The Crusaders were halted by a frontal archery assault and then surrounded. On the fourth day the desperate Crusaders made a final effort to break the encirclement, and at the end of a day of slaughter the senior knights fled the field. The Turks then assaulted the Christian camp and decimated the remaining infantry.

Kilij Arslan repeated his success against a second army under the command of Count William of Nevers, although the count made it easier for him due to his naïveté and tactical blunders. The Crusaders set out from Ankara and went south on a direct route for Jerusalem. This took them across the harsh dry lands of central Anatolia, which severely weakened them. The Turks had poisoned every water source and the pilgrimage now became a death march as the army struggled through the desert. Then Kilij Arslan struck. The infantry was abandoned by its knights and rapidly annihilated. The knights who had fled the battle were then duped by local guides who left them out in the desert.

Kilij Arslan completed his atonement for the failures of Nicaea and Doryaleum when he crushed a third Crusader army. This, led by William of Aquitaine, arrived at Heraclea in September 1101. This time the knights did not abandon their infantry, but this made no difference and only William and a handful of companions escaped the debacle.

Some Latin chroniclers suggest that Emperor Alexius had informed the Turks of the Crusader armies' progress and there may be a germ of truth in this. Maintaining the balance of power between the Turks and the Crusaders was a key strategic objective if the Byzantines were to maintain a presence in Anatolia – an important source of both taxes and recruits for the army – and to reclaim their northern Syrian possessions. What is more certain is that *if* these vast Latin armies had reached Palestine both Aleppo and Damascus may very well have fallen to the Crusaders, and there would have been no Muslim bridgehead remaining in the Levant.

26 Crak De Chevaliers, Syria, twelfth century

Do not let your strong defences and fortresses deceive you and make you conceited. With this sincere advice, I may add this also very clearly that even if Alamut were one of the fortresses of the heavens, I could level it to the ground by the grace of God.

The Sultan Malikshah writing to the Assassin Grand Master Hasan-i-Sabbah.

The destruction by Kilij Arslan of the second wave of Crusaders left Outremer with a manpower problem. Local levies could be raised, and indeed many local Syrians and Turks were still to be found in the ranks of the Latins even at the death of the kingdom in 1291, but it was not enough. The Crusaders therefore built extensively and they built well, because fortifications effectively tackled much of their problem of a lack of men and knights to defend the territories they had won.

The Muslims had some experience of artifice in fortification from the Byzantine castles and fortified cities they had taken from the Greeks but the technology employed and sheer size of structures such as Crak de Chevaliers would surely have inspired a degree of awe or least doubt over the ability of siege engines to bring down such a fortress. It seems likely that because of the highly mobile nature of first Arab and then later Turkish warfare, fortification was never

really that highly developed in the medieval Islamic world. Indeed, the Persian word used to describe Alamut, the greatest fortress of the Assassins sect, is *qal'a*, which like the Arabic *qasr* translates simply as 'fortified place' rather than castle per se. It is perhaps therefore better to view pre-Crusade Islamic fortresses as boltholes or refuges not dissimilar to the fortified villages of Umbria, Tuscany and the Marches of contemporary Italy. These were not structures designed, like a Western medieval castle, to strategically dominate a large area of fertile land. Nor were they built in a greatly 'scientific' manner like the huge concentric castles of the Crusaders. As a result siege warfare in the Middle East had not been well developed and relied to a great extent on the ability to starve out the occupiers of a castle. A well-prepared and fortified foe was, needless to say, a difficult proposition, especially for a large army consuming provisions at a faster rate than the besieged were.

Crak de Chevaliers is the epitome of Crusader castle building, with its enhancement of natural defences by the addition of immense moats, glacis and curtain walls and turrets, and the ability to form killing zones from its protruding towers. Its bakeries, cisterns and dry stores were immense and

any foe daring enough to want to challenge its walls with his mangonels would have very limited options for placing his siege artillery as there is barely a level patch of land surrounding the fearsome Hospitaller stronghold.

The Muslims would only reach such levels of sophistication in fortification under the Mamluk sultans of Egypt, in response to the two-front war they had to fight in Syria against the Crusaders and the Mongols. Evidence of their rapidly-acquired skills of fortification can also be seen in Crak de Chevaliers in Sultan Baybars's addition of a square tower to give extra protection for the access bridge.

27 Karak Castle, Jordan, twelfth century

The art of defending fortified places consists in putting off the moment of their reduction . . .
Frederick the Great.

The Franks fortified the coast with maritime castles, and coastal cities such as Tyre were rapidly ringed with defensive walls. It became clear almost immediately to the Kings of Jerusalem that possession of the Syrian coast was the key to the defence and survival of the Latin states. An offensive castle strategy was also undertaken. Castles such as Karak interrupted Muslim communications between Damascus, Egypt and Mecca, allowed for the pillaging of caravans, and could also act as a turnpike to extract fees for safe passage from merchants.

Of course an exposed inland castle, with a limited garrison, was always at risk of being enveloped and slowly starved out, however strong its walls might be. In classic castle warfare, as practised with exemplary skill by the Crusaders of Syria in the twelfth century at least until King Guy's loss of the field army at the Battle of Hattin in 1187, the defenders of a fortified place aimed simply to hold out until the arrival of the kingdom's field army. This was a lesson that Frederick the Great still stressed when instructing his generals in 1747.

In fact Karak became the archetypal offensive castle. After it came into the possession of Reynald of Châtillon in 1176 he used it as his base for attempts to sack Mecca itself and for raids into the Red Sea and against the port of Jeddah. Reynald's strategy, though commonly condemned by historians, may also be viewed as the only logical aggressive or expansionist outlet for the Crusaders as their little kingdom was hemmed in by the Mediterranean on one side, by an increasingly

powerful Muslim foe to its east, and with Egypt a newly reinvigorated power under Sultan Saladin.

Karak fell to Saladin's nephew in 1188. Two previous sieges had ended in failure, the first of these included the legendary withholding of bombardment by Saladin upon a tower in which the newly wed Humphrey of Toron was spending the first night of his marriage with Isabella of Jerusalem. During the second siege the Muslims attempted to fill the giant ditches surrounding the castle as they attempted to get mangonels close enough to make an impact on its walls. The third siege took several months to bring the garrison to surrender, but could be continued in the confidence that no relief army was coming to push Saladin's men from the walls as the Crusader field army had been smashed by the Sultan at Hattin.

28 The Great Seal of the Grand Masters of the Knights Templar, showing the order's symbol of two knights on one horse, c. 1158

And this place is very dreadful and dangerous. Seven rivers flow from this town of Bashan and great reeds grow along these rivers and many tall palm trees stand about the town like a dense forest. This place is terrible and difficult of access for here live fierce pagan Saracens who attack travellers at the fords on these rivers. And lions are found here in great numbers. This place is near the River Jordan and a great watermeadow lies between the Jordan and the town of Bashan and the rivers flow from Bashan into the Jordan and there are many lines of that place.

Daniel, a Russian Abbot of the twelfth century,
describing the dangers of Palestine to pilgrims.

The Templars emerged probably in the year 1118, and would within two years begin to provide active protection of the pilgrim routes that led to Jerusalem. William of Tyre tells us that the first knights to take the vows of poverty, chastity and obedience that marked out this unusual order of monk-soldiers were Hugh of Payns and Godfrey of Saint Omer. The two knights were blessed in their venture by the Patriarch of Jerusalem. The King of Jerusalem, Baldwin II, granted the nascent movement a property on the south side of the Temple Mount. It is unclear whether the two knights meant simply to adopt a penitential way of life and that the role of warriors of God came later and or whether Baldwin recognised with some immediacy how useful such men would be in bolstering the stretched military resources of the Latin Kingdom. Even the small contingent of around thirty companions who joined Hugh and Godfrey would be of value during a period of considerable peril for the Crusaders as minor Muslim princes of the region finally began to take up arms against the invaders. In January 1120 an assembly of prelates and secular leaders held in Nablus issued a series of decrees that probably included the formalising of the Templar order.

Nothing quite like the Templars had existed in Christendom before. Certainly the Knights Hospitaller predated them, but their vows were directed at providing shelter and care for pilgrims rather than directly confronting the enemies of Outremer on the battlefield. One possible inspiration for the Templar order could in fact have been the *ghazis* of Islam. These fighters for the faith would leave safe homelands to fight on the borders of Islam against the pagan Turks or Byzantines, and live together as communities in *ribats*, fortified Muslim monasteries. In eleventh and twelfth-century Syria there were also *futuwwa* or brotherhoods such as the Nubuwwiya, whose central principle was the eradication of Shiism from the region. These brotherhoods were associations of young men, with distinct ranks and rites to mark the attainment of manhood. Most were followers of holy men and had cult practices.

The discipline that the Templars showed within their strict hierarchy was directly related to the religious nature of their brotherhood. This reflected the ecclesiastical discipline based on celibacy and rejection of worldly honours and desires that had been instilled by Urban II into the Church and by the Cluniac philosophy of Gregory the Great. The monkish lifestyles of the grand masters would have recommended itself to the clerics of Cluny. At the birth of the order these knights were the ideal Crusaders. They fought to free the Holy Land but also retained a higher ideal of the 'other' Jerusalem, the celestial city that existed above the ordinary gore and dirt of this earth.

 ## The Walls of Malta, sixteenth century

Then the two masters said to the envoy: 'We command you to speak it'. And he said, that, since they commanded him, he would repeat it to them. Then the two masters caused him to be told in Arabic, that he was to come and speak with them the next day at the Hospital; which he did. Then the two masters said to him that his lord was a very bold man, to dare to send such harsh language to the king.

The Lord of Joinville describing how little fear the Grand Masters of the Hospital and Temple had for the deadly Assassins creed and the veiled threats of their envoys.

The Templars complemented quite neatly the activities of the Hospitallers who had been providing shelter and medical care for pilgrims from about 1080. The origins of this order seem to have been initially more directly linked to the monastic life than the more martial Templars, and their first base was in an annex of the monastery of Santa Maria Latina in Jerusalem. After the Crusader conquest in 1099 they very quickly gained royal favour and this patronage allowed the order to obtain properties throughout the kingdom. Through this both political influence and wealth came quickly to the order. By the 1130s the Hospitallers had taken on a military role entirely similar to that of the Templars, and by the time of the Second Crusade in 1147–9 the idea of military-monastic orders had become a natural aspect of Outremer's Latin Christian life.

Certainly the orders were needed, even in the early twelfth century when the Crusaders had tamed the Fatimids in the field through the series of defeats that they had inflicted upon the Egyptian Caliphate and were protected from any organised riposte from the Saljuqs due to the chaos that continued to shake the Baghdad Caliphate. There were still attacks on pilgrims and according to a letter from the Prior of the Holy Sepulchre in the 1120s the Kingdom was so insecure that no man would dare to venture beyond the walls of Jerusalem.

Both the Templars and the Hospitallers constantly appealed to the faithful of Europe for funds to support their works, and largesse flowed freely to the orders and funded their castle building and recruitment of local troops to garrison these bulwarks and to supplement the small number of knights. Both orders also allied with the Italian maritime republics that had established themselves in each of the Crusader states, and soon enough became economic and political rivals. As we will see below, whilst in the early part of Outremer's history the Crusaders showed a cohesion very much lacking among their enemies, as the Kingdom aged fatal fault lines emerged between its defenders.

30 Portrait of Alof de Wignacourt, the Grand Master of the Knights of Saint John, Caravaggio, c. 1607

The Templars are most excellent soldiers. They wear white mantles with a red cross, and when they go to the wars a standard of two colours called balzaus is borne before them. They go in silence. Their first attack is most terrible. In going they are the first, in returning the last . . .

A description of the Templars by an unknown pilgrim c. 1187.

The military orders were an immense source of strength for the Crusader kingdom for the simple reason that Crusaders came and went, and kings and higher lords were commonly ephemeral warriors and no more than visitors to the shores of the Levant. Once their pilgrim vows were complete and they had 'stood where Christ had stood' they left the Holy Land and returned to their European possessions. The Templars, Hospitallers and from 1198 the Teutonic Knights, along with the other 'minor' orders such as that of Saint Lazarus for leprous knights, were simply not going home, and in fact drew money and men from Europe to Outremer. The treatment by Muslim war leaders of any member of the military orders who was captured in battle is evidence of the obstinate nature of these knights. Even Saladin, with his enviable reputation for clemency, executed Templar and Hospitaller knights that had the temerity to surrender to him.

Chivalry and heroic *geste* or deeds were one thing, but the survival of Latin Jerusalem was more dependent on a grinding war of defence, attrition and raids than upon further quixotic conquests. Professional soldiers and the immense bulwarks of defence that the military orders created to house them cost money, and as noted above and as will be seen later in our story, the Italian maritime republics were also stalwart defenders of Outremer but very much expected to reap the rewards of Mammon as well as those of salvation. More and more over the brief period of the Latin states' survival the military orders began to ally with Venice, Genoa or Pisa.

By the time of the Third Crusade there were distinct and antagonistic factions within the Crusader states with Pisa and Venice aligning with either of the most powerful military orders in order to maintain an advantage over their rival and to pressure weak kings. In his classic three-part history of Outremer Grousset described the slow unravelling of the Crusader Kingdom as *L'anarchie Musulmane et la Monarchie Franque*, *Monarchie Franque et Monarchie Musulman l'equilibre*, and *La Monarchie Musulmane et L'anarchie Franque*.

The military orders made a huge contribution to the initial success and cohesion of the Kingdom, but their machinations and rivalries ultimately added to the anarchy that tore Outremer apart once they were faced by a united and committed foe. The Muslim riposte to the Christian invasion of the Levant was slow to evolve, often halting and contradictory, but it eventually produced the Mamluk Sultanate, an army-state made up of the greatest warriors the world had yet seen.

A Muted Response?

③1 The *Minbar.* These examples are from the late medieval period

When they entered the court of the mosque, a man leapt out of the crowd, without exciting the attention of anyone, and approaching the emir Mawdud as though to call down a blessing on him and beg alms of him, seized the belt of his riding cloak and smote him twice with his poniard below the navel. One of the blows penetrated his flank and the other his thigh. As the Assassin struck his second blow swords fell upon him on every side and he was struck with every kind of weapon. His head was cut off that it might be known who it was but he could not be recognised, so a fire was kindled for him and he was thrown upon it.

Ibn Al-Qalanasi, a contemporary chronicler of the Crusades
period and citizen of Damascus.

The *minbar*, or pulpit, directly indicated the sultan's legitimacy as the defender of the faith, and the *khutba* or Friday sermon that commonly acted as a hagiography of the sultan was given from it. In Baghdad in 1111 there were disturbances of the Friday prayers by Syrian refugees in Baghdad that included dragging the imam from the *minbar* in the main mosque and then smashing it to pieces. This was a powerful form of political protest and may have acted as a catalyst for the first expedition to the Levant sponsored by Sultan Muhammad in 1111. Muhammad was also able to act as the wars over possession of Baghdad finally burnt themselves out with the death of Sultan Berkyaruq and the absence of any further challengers to his reign.

This said, another powerful motivation for the sultan to commit forces to Palestine and Syria was to bring

Damascus and Aleppo back into the Saljuq Empire's embrace. Both cities were reluctant, however, to rejoin the family firm, and Prince Ridwan closed the gates of Aleppo to Mawdud, the new governor of Mosul and Muhammad's general. The sultan's army then devastated the countryside surrounding Aleppo to a far greater extent than the Crusaders had ever done. Nothing else was achieved and Joscelin of Tel-Bashir was even able to bribe off some of the senior emirs to speed along the falling apart of the whole venture.

Mawdud returned in 1113 with orders to bring all the emirs of Syria together to launch an assault on the *Franj*, but the order deliberately excluded Aleppo from this union of Muslims. Mawdud established himself in Damascus, which was under the rule of Tughtigin, who was acting as *atabeg*, or guardian to a Saljuq prince in his minority.

Mawdud fell to the daggers of the Ismaili Assassins as he was leaving the great mosque of Damascus, and the sultan's ambitions once again disintegrated. The murder was almost certainly sponsored by Ridwan of Aleppo, but Tughtigin's complicity cannot be ruled out. He lacked a caliphal diploma to rule Damascus and would have feared the possibility of Mawdud removing him under the sultan's authority.

Up to this point the expedition had been reasonably successful. Near Tiberias it had met and defeated King Baldwin and Roger of Antioch, through a series of charges across the bridge of al-Sinnabrah. After the battle the forces of Damascus did not march on with Mawdud to attempt the capture of any towns, and instead headed to the environs of Jerusalem and Jaffa to plunder. The lord of Damascus helped Mawdud rein in the Franks, but he would do no more, for fear of Baghdad's man gaining a foothold in Syria. This would be the pattern of the early Muslim riposte to the Crusaders – every success was hobbled by a lack of unity and vested interests that denied the victors any chance to land a really significant blow.

32 The Great Mosque of Damascus, c. 705

Dare you slumber in the blessed shade of safety, where life is as soft as an orchard flower?
How can the eye sleep between the lids at a time of disasters that would waken any sleeper?
While your Syrian brothers can only sleep on the backs of their chargers or in vulture's bellies!
Abu l-Musaffar al-Abiwardi, a poet of the twelfth century.

The sultan's final expedition set out in 1115. This time Damascene resistance to Baghdad's reach was overt. Damascus, Aleppo and Crusader Antioch allied against the sultan's forces. The sultan's commander, Bursuq, pushed towards Antioch, but Roger mobilised early, upon intelligence from Edessa, and met with the forces of Aleppo and Damascus, as well as those of Il-Ghazi of Mardin not far from Hama.

Baldwin then arrived with the armies of Jerusalem and of Tripoli. As the king, such support of Roger, who was technically his vassal, was expected but Baldwin was also a tough and responsible monarch and his arrival was enough to make Bursuq abandon a planned attack on Roger's camp.

Bursuq then retreated and this was enough to split the junior emirs, who had joined the expedition in the expectation of plunder, from his command. The composite and tribal

nature of Turkish armies was another weakness that acted against a concerted campaign of confrontation with the Crusader states. Bursuq took the field again at Tal Danith, but it took only the army of Antioch and of Edessa to defeat him. His troops were surprised whilst they watered their horses in the Orontes River and he was decisively beaten. For the Syrian-Turkish princes, the campaign's result was that the status quo ante returned and they remained free of interference from Baghdad. Usama Ibn-Munqidh, an Arab warrior of Shayzar who fought hard against the Crusaders in several campaigns, did not appear at all surprised or outraged by the 'stratagem by the governor of Aleppo' of allying with Roger. Baghdad's involvement in the affairs of the Levant were finished. It perhaps seems perverse that the main agent of resistance to the Crusaders in the early part of the twelfth century, given its actions in 1111, 1113, and 1115, was in fact Tughtigin's Damascus. Damascus made treaties with Latin Jerusalem, but in fact the city continued to strongly resist the Crusaders in southern Syria. Tughtigin took on a protective occupation of Tyre in 1112 and his forces fought alongside the Fatimids at Ascalon in 1118.

The Mantle of Roger II of Sicily, with Islamic Motifs, probably produced in Cairo, c. 1133–1134

33

But why did they not dare? Why did so many people and so many kingdoms fear to attack our little kingdom and our humble people? Why did they not gather from Egypt, from Persia, from Mesopotamia, and from Syria at least a hundred times a hundred-thousand fighters to advance courageously against us, their enemies?

From the *Historia Hierosolymitana* of Fulcher of Chartres.

The Mantle of the Norman King Roger II of Sicily carries motifs of lions attacking camels and is very much in the style of fine Fatimid-period Egyptian textiles. The style is also that of the *khila* or robe of honour that would be bestowed upon servants and allies of the Fatimid Caliph who had performed great deeds. Tughtigin, the *atabeg* of the Prince of Damascus, the most orthodox Sunni city in Syria, received just such a robe from the Shia state of Egypt for his tenacious resistance against the *Franj*. The *khila* also served as the ruler's vow of *aman*, or protection, and by this act the Fatimids were stating that an understanding of mutual defence existed between the two states.

Indeed Damascus had been being wooed by the Fatimid *wazir* al-Afdal since 1102 with letters requesting the help of Damascus's army in, 'the Holy War for Muslim lands and for Muslim folk'. He

repeated these appeals in 1105, as he sought to form a united front with his Sunni enemies against the new foe. In August of the same year al-Afdal moved on Ramla, and Saljuq troopers from Damascus came in support of his force and were almost enough to bring about victory. King Baldwin had to drive these Turks from his army's rear before moving forward to engage the Fatimids. He held the field at the end of the day but the victory was inconclusive, if bloody, as the Egyptians managed a well-ordered retirement to their redoubt of Ascalon.

The Muslim powers in Syria and Palestine remained unable to defeat the Franks in a pitched battle or to gain a definitive advantage over them but Fatimid raids on Crusader lands did, however, distract the Franks from their reduction of the coastal cities of Palestine and this should not be underestimated. Raiding, in a fragile agrarian economy such as Syria, was as likely to bring an area under control as was a full campaign, or at least make its continued occupation untenable. Combined with al-Afdal's Damascene diplomacy which saw Damascus fighting alongside the Egyptians at Ascalon in 1118, and the efforts of the Fatimid fleet, this was enough to keep at least some of the cities of the coast under Muslim control for the early part of the twelfth century.

The Assassins' Creed Game and Media, twentieth to twenty-first century

The damage caused by the Batiniyya to the Muslim sects is greater than the damage caused them by the Jews, Christians and Magians; nay, graver than the injury inflicted on them by the Materialists and other non-believing sects; nay, graver than the injury resulting to them from the Antichrist who will appear at the end of time.

Abu-Mansur Abd-al-Kahir ibn Tahir al-Baghdadi. The Ismailis were known as the *Batiniyya*, as they claimed that there were hidden meanings, *batin*, in the Quran that only the enlightened could comprehend.

So, to a degree there was co-operation between the Shia and Sunni forces of Syria and Egypt against the Crusaders but this really just proved the old proverb, 'the enemy of my enemy is my friend'. It would take the outrages committed by a far more radical sect of Shia followers than the Fatimids to drive the Sunni Levant towards a cohesive and committed jihad. The Ismaili Assassins would be a catalyst for the jihad that began to ferment among the petty Turkish rulers of Syria and in the Jazira of northern Iraq.

The Nizar Ismaili creed had, early on, established themselves as a faction capable of controlling the weak and politically isolated prince of Aleppo, Ridwan. The large Shiite population in Aleppo had earlier caused Ridwan to take Fatimid allegiance as a means to shore up his domestic approval. The Ismailis seem to have presented themselves to Ridwan as 'fixers', who could take care of all his political and population concerns in return for the free use of Aleppo as a base for propagating their faith and for the chance to obtain some strong fortresses. The first killing was of Prince al-Dawla of Homs, one of Ridwan's political enemies, and an ally of Damascus. The assassination of Mawdud in Damascus in 1113 kept both Ridwan and the Ismailis safe from interference from Baghdad but then as Ridwan lay dying in December 1113, Ibn al-Khashab, the Sunni *qadi* of Aleppo and Ibn Badi, the leader of the city militia, gathered supporters and as many of the city's militiamen as they could trust together. During the night, they spread out through the city, seizing and killing as many of the Nizari Ismailis as they could find. The *qadi* knew that he did not have the manpower to take on his Turkish overlords, but he hoped to deprive Ridwan's son and heir, Alp Arslan, of the support base his father had relied on and by virtue of this to force the young prince, who was only 16, to depend on the Sunni body politic. The *qadi*'s policy seemed initially to be a success and Alp Arslan, perhaps sensing which way the wind was blowing, added his support to the anti-Nizari campaign. The Ismaili leader was killed and about 200 of his followers were also executed. But then under the prince's guidance

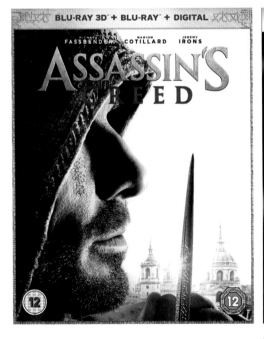
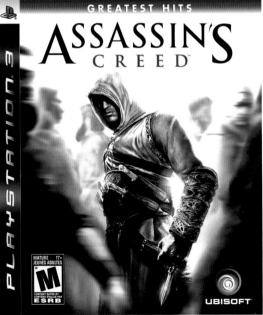

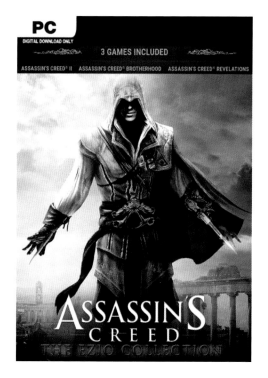
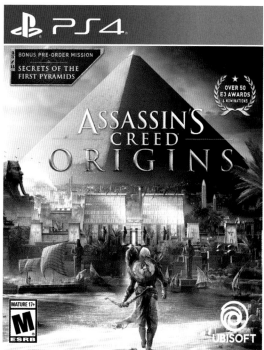

the purge quickly became a bloodbath, as these things are wont to do, and was used as a cloak for the destruction of all possible opposition to the new reign. Certainly, several more Nizaris were executed by being thrown off the citadel, but two of Alp Arslan's brothers were also executed and officers and palace functionaries were included in the indiscriminate slaughter. Alp Arslan was eventually killed by one of his close servants named Lu Lu, in September 1114, as he slept. Aleppo was now under the rule of Lu Lu and an infant son of Ridwan. The governor of the city of Mardin saw an opportunity.

35 The Arab Horse. Timeless

The best life is that of the man who holds his horse's rein in Allah's way and flies on its back to the places from whence he hears a war cry or the clatter of arms, seeking martyrdom or slaughter on the battlefield . . .

From the Hadith, The Book of Jihad.

Roger of Antioch acted quickly upon the death of Ridwan and took all of the major fortresses ringing the city in preparation for its reduction in the same year. In response to this threat the now *atabeg* Lu Lu called on Il-Ghazi of Mardin for support. Il-Ghazi quickly occupied Aleppo and was supported by the Sunni *ulama* of the city. These same Sunni clerics had been the most voluble of all in their calls for jihad against the Franks ever since the first refugees from the coastal cities taken by the Crusaders had flooded into Aleppo. It was also these same men who had started the pogrom against the Ismailis of Aleppo of 1113.

Il-Ghazi's experience as a cavalry soldier and leader was extensive, but what was happening at Aleppo was significant for other reasons. As at Maarrat al-Numan, the Sunni leaders of the *ulama* had taken control of a key resistance point to the *Franj*. A *qadi's* religious authority was largely subordinated to the political authority of his Saljuq governor. Therefore calls for jihad from the *ulama* were always likely to fail against the indifference of a Turkish hegemony that had a strong disdain for the non-military intelligentsia. The difference here was that jihad was a perfect stalking horse for the territorial ambitions of a prince like Il-Ghazi, who was now free of fear of interference from Baghdad.

Roger of Antioch was beginning a siege of Aleppo as Il-Ghazi arrived in the city. The *ulama* of the city therefore made immediate calls for the whole city to follow them, along with Il-Ghazi, in jihad against the Crusaders. It was just the stirrings of a response, but a start had been made. Ibn al-Qalanasi wrote of how:

Il-Ghazi made his emirs swear that they would fight bravely, that they would hold their positions, that they would not retreat, and that they would give their lives for the jihad. The Muslims were then deployed in small waves, and managed to take up night-time positions alongside Roger's troops. At daybreak the Franj *suddenly saw the Muslim banners approach, surrounding them on all sides. The qadi, Ibn al-Khashab advanced astride his mare, and gestured with one hand urging our forces into battle. Seeing him one of our soldiers shouted contemptuously, 'have we come all the way from our home country to follow a turban?' But the qadi marched towards the troops, moved through their ranks, and addressed them, trying to rouse their energy and lift their spirits, delivering a harangue so eloquent that men wept with emotion and felt great admiration for him. Then they charged. Arrows flew like a cloud of locusts.*

At the end of the battle, known in the West as *Ager Sainguinis* or the Field of Blood, Roger was dead and his men and horses, the entire field army of Antioch, according to Ibn al-Qalanasi, looked like stretched-out hedgehogs, such was the volume of arrows the men of Il-Ghazi had poured into them as they sped by on their steeds. Needless to say the horse was a revered beast among the Turks, and even the Turcomen had at least two warhorses in their retinue along with a palfrey for riding to war, and Il-Ghazi's *askari* would have been aboard fleet mares. By the time of the Mamluk sultanate every trooper had stabled, well-fed horses capable of carrying a fully armoured cavalryman at high speed and of cantering without any need of rein control as its master shot arrow after arrow from the saddle.

Backyard Jihad and Détente

36 A Chalice carved from Rock Crystal. Fatimid workmanship with later Parisian mounting. c. 1100 and 1225–1250

This is war,
And the man who shuns the whirlpool to save his life shall grind his teeth in penitence.
This is war,
And the infidel's sword is naked in his hand,
Ready to be sheathed again in men's necks and skulls.
This is war,
And he who lies in the tomb at Medina seems to raise his voice and cry: 'O sons of Hashim!'

Al-Abiwardi, a twelfth-century Iraqi poet.

It was a great victory and it seemed to herald the emergence of the kind of union between faith and military action that had brought Islam its early conquests. The Sunni world had lost this union during its subjugation by professional Turkish military men, and the Fatimids had fallen under the power of their own *wazirs*. Their state became both weak and yet, ironically, dominated by the military, losing all of its fervour.

However, Il-Ghazi's men failed to follow up on their victory and dispersed for plunder, the prince himself dying in 1122 of alcoholic cirrhosis. It seemed as if nothing had changed but in fact Antioch had been crippled and Edessa's existence began to look increasingly parlous. There was also a definitive hardening of attitudes towards the foe on both sides. This piece of Fatimid crystal would most likely have entered the West via Sicily or Venice rather than across the Palestine

to Syria 'front line'. Some Franks might take on oriental ways as we have seen with Tancred, but the Crusaders' attitudes to Islam remained fixed, antagonistic and generally uninterested in comprehending the faith they opposed. Equally the Turks began more and more to take on the mantle of jihad and to be less accepting of the Crusader presence in lands that had been part of the Saljuq Empire.

Il-Ghazi's son, Suleiman, was quickly removed by his cousin Balak, who usurped the Aleppan throne after a whirlwind campaign of blockade and crop burning. Balak soon gave his new subjects something to cheer when he captured Joscelin, the new count of Edessa, near the city of Saruj. Then in 1123, he went one better and bagged Baldwin II near the walls of Edessa. Joscelin was rescued by Armenians disguised as monks and then daringly crossed the Euphrates on inflated wineskins, but Baldwin II failed to escape and remained a captive.

In 1124 Balak, the new hero of Muslim Syria, received an appeal for aid against the Crusaders from a besieged Tyre, but was killed by an arrow shot from Manbj, a fortress of a rival emir that he was besieging. He is said to have pulled it from his neck with the words, 'that blow will be fatal for all the Muslims,' and then fell dead. His rule had been short but it helped nourish the lore of jihad that was continuing to grow in northern Syria and in the Jazira. His cenotaph was inscribed with his deeds in the Holy War and contemporary writers tell us of warriors who, 'bravely make it their duty to fight with heroism . . . they spill their blood for the Holy War'.

37 The Great Mosque of al-Nuri in Mosul before and after its destruction by the Islamic State, late twelfth century and 2019

The lord of Mosul, Qasim al-Dawla Aqsunqur al-Bursuqi was killed in Mosul. The Batinis assassinated him in the congregational Mosque, when he was at Friday prayers with the people. The previous night he had seen in his dream that several dogs attacked him. He killed some but the rest did him some harm. He related this dream to his companions and they advised him not to leave the house for several days. He said, 'I shall not miss Friday prayers for anything . . .'

Ibn al-Athir, *The Perfect History.*

Baldwin obtained his freedom after the payment of a ransom to Timurtash, a second son of Il-Ghazi and Balak's successor in Aleppo. Baldwin then somewhat unchivalrously gathered together some Bedouin and besieged Aleppo. Once again the 'turban' Ibn al-Khashab stepped into the breach and conducted the defence of the city. Having failed to summon help from Timurtash, he sent instead to al-Bursuqi, the governor of Mosul; and the arrival of al-Bursuqi and his forces at Aleppo was enough to make Baldwin hurriedly retire in January 1125.

Al-Bursuqi immediately began to threaten Edessa, but his Turks were defeated by Joscelin and Baldwin at the Battle of Azaz on 13 June 1125. The Crusaders managed to close on the Turks before they could loose their arrows, and the encounter soon became a close-quarters fight with lance and sword which the Turks were not capable of winning. Baldwin beat the new Prince of Aleppo again at Marj al-Suffar in January 1126, though it was a close-run thing and the Turks inflicted severe damage on the Crusaders with their archery before the king managed to organise a charge that closed the battle.

Al-Bursuqi was killed by a gang of Ismaili Assassins shortly after as he left the great mosque in Mosul.

Perhaps the dogs of his nightmare were made flesh. Ibn al-Khashab had suffered the same fate the summer before outside Aleppo's great mosque.

Aleppo was politically rudderless once again, and we can see once again how assassination was a potent political weapon in the medieval period, as so much in the political arena depended on individuals and their actions. It commonly caused the complete breakdown of order in any state or principality, as it had with the Saljuq Empire in 1092. Yet, despite having to pay tribute to Bohemond II, the new ruler of Antioch, and being constantly threatened by Baldwin, Aleppo did not fall. This was primarily because the princes of Mosul viewed it now as their protectorate – just as it had been al-Bursuqi's 'second city' when he was governor of Mosul. Freed of the fear of interference in their affairs by Baghdad after the failure of the sultan's sponsored expeditions, they now applied themselves more to Syrian than Iraqi affairs. Antioch had also not recovered militarily from the Battle of *Ager Sanguinis*, and Baldwin was frequently embroiled with Damascene affairs, as well as the reduction of the coastal cities.

38   The Arsenal of Venice, twelfth to fifteenth century

Who hath taken this counsel against Tyre, that was formerly crowned, whose merchants were princes, and her traders the nobles of the earth?

Isaiah 23:8

The disaster at *Ager Sanguinis* forced Baldwin to call upon the Venetians for help. In return they were offered trade privileges throughout the kingdom, but before the promised reinforcements could arrive Baldwin had been captured by Balak. Despite this, the Venetians sailed to Tyre where their fleet of 100 warships began a blockade to match a landward siege of the city by the Franks in February 1124.

The city surrendered on terms on 7 July 1124 and the Venetian fleet was the key to its fall. Tyre was virtually an island and could only be approached on a narrow causeway; it was also surrounded by three strong concentric walls. Troops from Damascus defended the causeway but there was little they could do to stop the bombardment of the city from the Venetian ships. The garrison fought bravely and used hooks to turn over Crusader battering rams, but with the failure of the Fatimid fleet to break the Venetian blockade, and the death of Balak, resistance was seen as futile and the Damascene troops were allowed to depart for their own city as part of the surrender agreement.

The Venetians took a third of the city as their share. By 1131, Pisa had also established its own little colony. The martial capability of the Italian maritime republics in the twelfth century is very clear, but what also see in this period is their material influence on the process that was

already taking place in Europe of the romanticizing of Crusading and of the 'East'. The troubadours and returning knights from the First Crusade were elemental to the creation of 'chivalry' and the propagation of myths of comely oriental virgins and *houris*, and assassins lurking in the shadows and using magic to achieve their kills, but it was the products of the East that now began to enter Europe via the Syrian Crusader ports in large amounts that really cemented the reputation of the mystical lands of the Levant and beyond. Compared to the merchandise available in the West, the imported products of Islam were fine beyond all measure and this is reflected in the number of Persian words that made their way into European languages along with these goods of desire – jasmine, crimson, taffeta, musk, candy, saffron and the ultimate extravagance, pyjamas. The shipyards of Venice, Pisa and Genoa produced the galleys that made the taking of the coast possible, and the same yards produced merchantmen at an astonishing rate in order to bring luxuries, staples, and myths to the West.

39 A Reliquary Casket made from Fatimid rock crystal plaques, c. 1200

As he sat upon his horse in readiness for the attack, splendid in red and gold arms and armour, girt with the sword of his ancestor Ali and wielding two lances, the animal pranced and one spear fell. The evil omen turned to good when the prince recited the tale of Moses's staff, thrown down to confute the wizards of Pharaoh; and the narrator to whom the verse was addressed saluted the light of prophecy which laid the meaning of the Holy Book open to his lord and master, the Son of the Messenger of God, the Imam of the Community.

The Crown Prince Ismail of the Fatimid Dynasty, as described by the religious judge *Qadi* al-Askar al-Marwarrudhi before an assault on Kharijite rebels in 947.

Reliquaries commonly hold the often desiccated and crumbling remains of saints. The magnificent and warlike Fatimid state and elite of the tenth century had also crumbled almost to dust by the 1130s. The army had been decimated in 1123 at the Battle of Yibneh during a campaign to recapture Jaffa. Its massed ranks of Sudanese foot-archers presented the Franks with a static target for their charge and the light Berber cavalrymen were not capable of defending the infantry. The battle only lasted an hour and a hurriedly-launched Damascene diversionary tactic did not distract the Franks from their task of butchery.

The Egyptian navy was fading from the scene too. After the fall of Tyre the Fatimid fleet is barely mentioned in the chronicles, excepting some piratical raids in the 1150s. Apart from occasional raids from Ascalon, little was heard from the army either. William of Tyre dismissed the Egyptians as 'effeminates', but this is far from the whole truth. In fact the Fatimids' withdrawal from the war for Syria

was not a direct result of Frankish victories per se, and their one victory in the second Battle of Ramla had at least exposed one weakness of the Frankish state – there were simply not enough Latin soldiers.

Egyptian isolationism in the period immediately after 1125 was, in fact, a result of sustained political crises. The Ismaili Assassins murdered the *wazir* al-Afdal in 1121, possibly with the connivance of the Fatimid caliph, and tipped the already fragile state into a cycle of political murders and intrigues as *wazirs* and caliphs competed for the allegiances of army factions. In 1130 the caliph, al-Amir, was also killed by the Assassins. Egypt turned in on itself and became largely irrelevant to the Crusaders until they sought its conquest three decades later. In fact they should have acted in 1130 when the state was ripe for conquest and Damascus was distracted by a succession crisis. As would become apparent during the contests with Nur al-Din and Saladin, without Egypt the Crusader Kingdom was an isolated colony, especially given the growing and overt animosity of Byzantium in the north and the threat of the Turks of the Jazira to Outremer's east.

40 A Damascus Sword Maker. 'Whose swords were once considered the finest in the world', c. 1900

Paradise has one-hundred grades which Allah has reserved for the Mujahedeen who fight in his cause, and the distance between each grade is like the distance between the heavens and the Earth.

From the Hadith. The Book of Jihad.

Tughtigin, the *atabeg* of Damascus, died in February 1128. During his final years he had involved himself with the Ismaili Assassins, even to the extent of employing hundreds of known Ismailis in his army. The Franks controlled the entire coast, Egypt was finished with the war and Damascus nearly fell to the Ismailis as Tughtigin breathed his last.

The Assassins failed to take control of Damascus simply because the Sunni revival in northern Syria, based around the embryonic jihad of Il-Ghazi and Balak, and the continuing involvement of the *ulama* in martial and government affairs, was now also taking place further south. Tughtigin's heir Buri moved quickly following the old man's death. He surprised and executed his father's *wazir*, a known sympathiser with the Ismaili Assassins, and employed the city's militia to purge the city of the creed. Ibn al-Qalanasi tells us that 'by the next morning, the quarters and streets of the city were cleared of the *Batinis* and the dogs were yelping and quarrelling over their limbs and corpses'.

The Ismailis attempted to exact their revenge through Baldwin by gifting him their castle of Banyas, which lay close to Damascus on the Jerusalem road. Baldwin gathered together forces from Jerusalem, Edessa, Antioch, the coastal cities and from the Knights Templar and began to plunder right up to Damascus's walls. Buri scraped together a force formed from nomadic Turcomen and Arabs of the region, with his *askari* and that of the Prince of Hama as a core.

He intercepted the Franks at the wooden bridge six miles from Damascus. He managed to get his Arab auxiliaries on all sides of the Franks and tried to break up the Crusader column with flying raids. Baldwin held his position and refused to offer battle knowing his knights and regular infantry would be capable of repelling the lightly-armed Arab and Turcomen horsemen. He also despatched a detachment to Hawrun, south of Damascus, to collect provisions for a siege of Damascus. Buri quickly dispatched a large number of his Arabs and Turcomen along with the *askari* of Hama to surprise this force.

The ambush was perfectly executed and many of the Crusaders were killed before they could even mount their warhorses. The Crusaders were unable to organise a charge because they were encumbered by baggage and supply mules and were riding their palfreys rather than their chargers. Their resistance eventually broke under the repeated Muslim assaults and William, the Constable of Jerusalem, fled the field with a party of knights. The remaining men-at-arms and infantry were either slaughtered or taken as slaves.

Buri attempted to engage the Crusaders at the wooden bridge, but Baldwin had had word of the disaster at Leja. The Muslims found only abandoned wounded men and a mass of injured horses at the bridge. The *askari* of Damascus pursued the Crusader rearguard and they killed a number of stragglers, but Baldwin managed a generally well-ordered retreat, and even hazarded later in the year another attempt to take Damascus but appalling weather ruined his plans. Damascus was the home of Syrian steel, its core economy, and its finest swords. Its conquest, or acquiescence, was central to the Crusader Kingdom's survival.

The Martyr and the Saint King

41 Greek Fire in the *Codex Græcus Matritensis Ioannis Skyllitzes*, twelfth century

> *I, having realized the effects wrought by Time, desire now by means of my writings to give an account of my father's deeds, which do not deserve to be consigned to Forgetfulness nor to be swept away on the flood of Time into an ocean of Non-Remembrance; I wish to recall everything . . .*
>
> Anna Comnena, *The Alexiad.*

Byzantium had gained a great deal from the First Crusade. Nicaea had been reclaimed by the empire, the high tide of the Turks' incursions into Asia Minor seemed to have been survived and the Byzantine navy had once more started to take control of at least the north-east Mediterranean following a massive naval rearmament programme, which produced three fleets of sophisticated warships, capable of delivering the 'secret' weapon of Greek Fire both above and below the waves, between 1090 and 1105.

The Crusaders may very well have wondered what *they* had gained from Byzantine aid. Given that Antioch's lands were continually threatened by the emperor's army and that, if the Latin chroniclers are to be believed, he was complicit in the destruction of the Crusading armies of 1101, then the Byzantines were an untrustworthy ally at best.

Alexius was certainly a great soldier, a superior tactician and a skilled politician. Maintaining the balance of power between the Turks and the Crusaders was a key strategic objective if he was to

keep a Byzantine presence in Anatolia, a vital source of both taxes for the empire and recruits for the army, and to reclaim his north Syrian possessions. Alexius also used the threat of the Franks in his negotiations with the Turks. Ibn al-Qalanasi wrote that Alexius, in an embassy to Baghdad in 1111, claimed to have so far impeded the Franks but that this impediment would cease if there was no effective Muslim response to the Latin advances. It is notable that a Muslim expedition was organised from Baghdad very shortly after this communication.

Alexius could of course easily salve his conscience with the taking of Edessa and Antioch by the Crusaders in contravention of their oaths to him, and with the acts of the Normans in particular. Their assaults on Byzantium predated the Crusade in the person of Guiscard and Bohemond, and Bohemond and Tancred continued to wound the Empire with Norman Antioch taking Tarsus, Adana and Massissa from the Byzantines. Indeed the assaults only ended with the failure of Bohemond's 1108 expedition to attempt the defeat of Alexius in Greece, and the great Norman's death shortly after.

By the 1130s the growing threat of the jihad that had grown from Mosul to Aleppo caused a realignment of alliances, with Raymond of Antioch recognising the Byzantine Emperor as his overlord, rather than the King of Jerusalem. It was a simple matter of survival as Byzantine strength in northern Syria had recovered to such extent that the Emperor John II was even able to begin a strident campaign against the Turks, and also reclaimed Tarsus and Adana from the Armenians. John also received the vassalage of Tripoli and of Edessa, and brought a Byzantine-Crusader army, with forces drawn from Antioch and Edessa, into Syria in the spring of 1138. He would find a very doughty opponent waiting for him on the battlefield.

 ## A Writing Case from the Jazira, with plaques showing the planets in character, thirteenth century

A man came to Allah's Messenger and said, 'guide me to such a deed that equals jihad'.
Muhammad replied, 'I do not find such a deed', and then he added, 'but can you while the Muslim fighter has gone for jihad, enter the mosque and pray without cease and observe a fast and never break your fast?'
The man said, 'but who can do that?'

From the Hadith, The Book of Jihad.

Buri of Damascus fell to the vengeful daggers of Ismaili Assassins who had worked their way into his close bodyguard. He was stabbed by two of his most trusted men in May 1131, as he was riding back from the baths. He survived the initial attack but succumbed to his wounds a year later.

The political value of the killing to the Assassins was minimal: the Sunni revival that was taking place in Syria was by now unstoppable. Damascus remained thoroughly orthodox in its religion and its politics, and a new Sunni champion emerged from the princes of the Jazira. He would come close to unifying all of Muslim Syria under him and to begin the destruction of Outremer.

Zangi, the Emir of Mosul, was without doubt somewhat unscrupulous and something of an adventurer. His later deeds raised him up to the title of *shahid* or martyr for the Faith but in his earlier career as the governor of Basra he had made war on the caliph, and had been rewarded by the sultan with Mosul and a free hand in the Jazira. The sultan also gave him diplomas of authority over the whole of Syria. He then moved quickly onto the politically rudderless Aleppo. He married the now thrice-wedded daughter of Ridwan and transferred his father's remains to the city – a highly symbolic act among Turkic peoples. Every Turkish prince in Syria knew that the union of Mosul and Aleppo under Zangi was a huge challenge to their continued independence.

Just before the Assassins' attack on him, Buri received letters from Zangi requesting the assistance of Damascus against the Franks. Five hundred men of Buri's *askari* were sent and joined the bodyguard of Hama, which was commanded by Buri's son. Zangi quickly created some trumped-up charges and imprisoned all the men of Damascus and Hama. He then seized Hama and demanded ransom from Damascus. Buri realised that he was dealing with the region's new strongman and he paid the ransom. The question now was whether Zangi would continue to grab land from his fellow Muslims or would he turn his ambitions to their Frankish neighbours. In truth he was as likely to do both.

In 1130, Bohemond II of Antioch was killed in battle. His widowed princess, despite being King Baldwin's daughter, then rebelled against a union of Antioch with the Kingdom of Jerusalem. Zangi raided Antioch's territory but he was stymied by the ever-active Baldwin II, who brought an army from Jerusalem to rein in his recalcitrant offspring. Baldwin's death in 1131 was a heavy blow to Outremer: none of his successors would ever bind the Latin states together as strongly as he had.

Zangi was distracted by Iraqi affairs during the early 1130s as the Caliph rebelled again, and was even able to defeat Zangi at Tikrit, where the *atabeg* would have lost his life if it had not been for a Kurd of the Ayyubid clan. For a time the caliph ruled over the sultan but by 1135 the scholar al-Ghazali's political formula of constituent authority belonging to the sultan, who gave only an oath of allegiance to the caliph, had been re-established.

Zangi could return to his designs on Damascus, and perhaps more.

43 The Ivory Cover of Queen Melisende of Jerusalem's Psalter, c. 1135

Tamer of the infidels and polytheists, leader in the holy war, helper of the armies, protector of the Muslims.

A contemporary dedication on an Aleppan building to the Mujahid Zangi.

Baldwin II was cursed with daughters. The usurping of his line's claim on the holiest throne in Christendom seemed the most likely outcome of the marriage of his oldest daughter Melisende to any magnate or king from Europe. He attempted to thwart this by investing her before his death, and after Melisende had given birth to a son, making her joint ruler along with the infant boy and her husband Fulk of Anjou. He also made Melisende the sole guardian for the future Baldwin III. This was a severe blow to the prestige of King Fulk when he ascended the throne as joint ruler with his wife in 1132, and in their reign we see significant cracks appearing in the unity of the Crusader state which a wily and forceful foe such as Zangi could exploit.

Zangi also had designs on Damascus. Tughtigin's mad son had taken the throne and was causing chaos but the emirs of the city frustrated Zangi in the field and a swift judicial murder of the insane prince and his replacement with a puppet put paid to any political opportunity that Zangi could act upon.

Zangi therefore switched to the easier option of grabbing cities and land from the Crusaders. By 1135, he had taken Atharib and Maarrat al-Numan without having to engage any Crusader field armies. He besieged the Frankish castle of Barin as part of a campaign against Muslim Homs. King Fulk and Raymond of Tripoli attempted to break the siege, but ran into a perfect ambush. Raymond was killed and the king fled for the cover of Barin. Zangi pressed the siege with a fierce mangonel bombardment and Fulk was captured as the castle fell.

Zangi released the king on easy terms as he needed to mobilise quickly to meet a new threat. As we have seen above, Byzantium was resurgent and pressing on Zangi's northern possessions.

In many ways the Crusaders were a huge advantage to Zangi in the campaign against John. He met the invasion of Muslim lands by the Byzantine-Tripoli forces with a rapid, wide-ranging and effective diplomatic operation, and an impressive local military response. He stirred up the Anatolian Turkish emirs into assaults on the emperor's recently regained territories, and ensured that there was enough turmoil produced in Baghdad by its *ulama*, to ensure that the sultan was chagrined into sending troops to his defence. His military clerks then sent letters to all the major cities still under Muslim control in Syria to come to his aid. He was able to do this because, despite his skulduggery against Damascus and his long campaigns against his Muslim neighbours over the last few years, he was now the hero of resistance to the *Franj* and to the emperor of the *Rum*, the Muslims' oldest enemy.

Jihad is a discrete action in Sunnism. Zangi was engaged in a project that was pan-Islamic, as the alliances he sought to form were aimed at defeating the *Franj*. Such coalitions were central to jihad. Zangi also got his propagandists to extol his virtues as a *ghazi* and Mujahid. Another key element

of jihad is that social justice must be exercised by its leaders. Zangi controlled his army through iron discipline, and crucified transgressors of his laws. Al-Isfahani tells us that Zangi was, 'tyrannical and indiscriminate', which in fact probably meant that he was harsh but fair and impartial in his justice.

So much for the ideological aspect of jihad: the Crusaders were about to feel its physical fury.

44 Counterweight Trebuchets, an invention of the early twelfth century

A holy man saw the dead Zangi in a dream and asked him, 'How has God treated you?' And Zangi replied, 'God has pardoned me because I conquered Edessa.'

Ibn al-Athir, *The Perfect History*.

Zangi travelled the length and breadth of Syria for 18 years on campaigns, and his charismatic leadership and personal bravery were the keys to keeping his army in the field. He was also a master of intrigue. His agents spread suspicion between the Byzantine-Crusader army's leaders during its unhappy retreat from his lands, and Turcomen border raids erupted all over John's lands.

Damascus was claimed by Zangi to be the key to defeating the Franks, and whilst this was certainly true, he was also as much interested in adding the riches of the city to his treasury as he was in the Holy War. He married the Prince of Damascus's mother and took Baalbek, the fortress that shielded the city's northern approaches. He secured the capitulation of troops holding out in the last tower with promises of safe passage. However, he quickly reneged on this pledge and had every man crucified.

Damascus resisted desperately with the city militia and a company of peasants taking the field against Zangi's professional soldiers, with predictable results. By March 1140 Zangi's troops

were closing on the city. The emirs of the city responded by gifting him a propaganda victory by allying with King Fulk, who received both monies and hostages from the Damascenes. It was enough to create stalemate in the contest over Damascus.

Fulk died in late 1143 and Queen Melisende took on the regency of the child king, Baldwin III. It was doubly unfortunate that Joscelin II of Edessa and Raymond of Antioch were also at loggerheads. The *ulama* called warriors to the jihad and in November 1144, knowing that Joscelin II was absent from Edessa, Zangi attacked the city. So, it may be that the deed for which Zangi is chiefly remembered was entirely opportunistic.

A swarm of Turcomen surrounded the city, intercepting all supplies and reinforcements. It was said that even birds dared not fly near, so absolute was the desolation made by the besiegers' weapons and so unblinking their vigilance. Counterweight trebuchets, a recent invention and a machine of enormous power capable of battering holes in even Edessa's thick walls, shot ceaselessly night and day. Sappers from far away Khurasan mined under the towers of the city's walls. Once the tunnels' supports were fired the walls crumbled.

William of Tyre tells us that the city fell rapidly because the population was made up of 'Chaldeans and Armenians, unwarlike men, scarcely familiar with the use of arms', and Queen Melisende's relief force never had a chance of reaching it in time.

Zangi moved rapidly to take Saruj, and Joscelin, who had fled to Turbessel, was fortunate that Zangi was briefly distracted once more by Damascene affairs. Then in early 1145 the Armenians of Edessa attempted to betray the city to Joscelin. Zangi marched north and rapidly crushed the conspiracy.

The guilty parties were crucified and the *shahid* moved onto quell a revolt at the fortress of Jabar on the Euphrates. Zangi was three months into a siege of the castle when he was stabbed to death by a Christian slave, as he lay drunk in his tent.

Camels carrying Projectile Weapons in Afghanistan, c. 1988

His treasures now the prey of others, by his sons and adversaries dismembered. At his death did his enemies ride forth, grasping the swords they dared not brandish whilst he lived . . .

Ibn al-Qalanasi's encomium to Zangi.

The Muslim army quickly dispersed and every commander made for a fortified city to claim a share of the spoils. The treasury was raided and Damascus took advantage of Zangi's death to seize Banyas once more. Raymond of Tripoli raided up to the walls of Aleppo.

Civil war and a regaining of the initiative by the *Franj* seemed the most likely outcome of Zangi's sudden death, but this did not occur and this was in part because Zangi's sons were each able to acquire a major city – Mosul for Sayf al-Din and Aleppo for Nur al-Din – and chose not to interfere with each other's ambitions in their respective spheres of the Jazira and Syria.

Nur al-Din was pious and reserved, and entirely more trustworthy than his father. His first concern was an attempt made by Joscelin II to recover Edessa. Nur al-Din's forced march from Aleppo, the sheer pace of which killed a number of horses, was enough, however, to deter Joscelin II from trying to hold onto the city. The speed with which Nur al-Din had established himself in north Syria made him an attractive proposition as a son in-law for Muin al-Din, the senior emir of Damascus, and a marriage contract to the emir's daughter was swiftly concluded. Muin al-Din then besieged both Sarkhad and Bosra, two fortresses that had rebelled against Damascus and had called on the Franks for aid.

Nur al-Din arrived at Bosra just before the Crusader army under the command of the 16-year-old Baldwin III. Nur al-Din showed himself to be the equal of his father. Camel-loads of arrows were brought to the battle, and their effect was just as deadly as the Afghani Mujahedeen's anti-tank grenade launchers carried by camels in the late 1980s. In projectile warfare logistics is everything, and camels can carry a heavy load.

Al-Qalanasi described Nur al-Din's first victory:

> *The combatants drew up eye to eye, and their ranks closed up to one another, and the askari of the Muslims gained the upper hand over the polytheists. They cut them off from watering places and pasture ground, they afflicted them with a hail of shafts and death-dealing arrows, they multiplied amongst them death and wounds, and set on fire the herbage on their roads and paths. The Franks, on the verge of destruction, turned in flight, and the Muslim knights and horsemen, seeing a favourable opportunity presented of exterminating them, made speed to slay and to engage in combat with them . . .*

The military union between Damascus and Aleppo was only one of convenience and was soon dissolved, but it remained a frightening prospect for the *Franj*, since dissent between Aleppo and Damascus had been pivotal to the Crusaders' success in the early years of their campaign.

Furthermore, the *Franj* now lacked the manpower to take on Nur al-Din. The annihilation of the Crusade of 1101, the second Battle of Ascalon, the Battles of al-Sinnabra and *Ager Sanguinis* and this last defeat at Bosra had made fielding an army increasingly difficult. There was a growing reliance on the military orders and mercenary forces, but the loss of territory to Zangi in the 1130s had made paying for such troops virtually impossible for the petty lords of Outremer.

A fresh influx of *Milites Christi* was required.

Of the Deaths of Great Armies and of Imaginary Realms

46 Coats of Arms, Cathedral of Saint Barbara, Kutná Hora, Czech Republic, fourteenth to nineteenth centuries

Canto l'arme pietose e 'l capitano, che 'l gran sepolcro liberò di Cristo.
Molto egli oprò co 'l senno e con la mano, molto soffrí nel glorioso acquisto;

I sing of the sacred armies, and the godly knight, that the great sepulchre of Christ did free,
much wrought his valour and foresight, and in that glorious war much suffered he;
Torquato Tasso, *La Gerusalemme Liberata*, 1575, Canto Primo, Verse I.

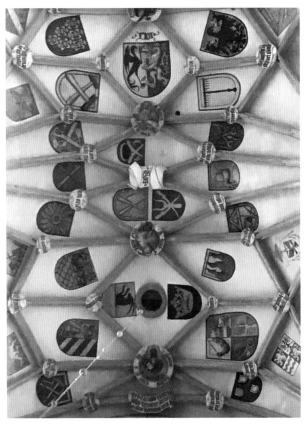

The fall of Edessa made for an unpleasant inauguration gift for the new pope, Eugenius III. He responded with a papal bull on 1 December 1145, and by the spring of 1146 King Louis of France made a commitment to a Crusade. The Holy Roman Emperor, Conrad III Hohenstaufen, also, if somewhat tardily, committed himself to the venture in December 1146. The Pope issued indulgences for the Crusade, though significantly these were also granted for an expedition into Slavic lands to Christendom's east and for the knights of the *Reconquista* in Spain. The divergence from the original notion of Crusading being solely the defence of Jerusalem to it being participation in any church-sponsored war, would be significant later.

Crusading was also becoming central to the new ideas of chivalry and of the right way of life for a knight.

Heraldry became central to the nobility of Crusader dynasties and to a knight's lineage. Falsification of family trees to place ancestors at key events during the Crusades and to boost a family's status and lineage was not uncommon and it has been suggested that Torquato Tasso, the author of *La Gerusalemme Liberata*, was perfectly amenable to bribery should a noble family want an ancestor to be placed at the taking of the Holy City in 1099.

The total destruction of the army of Conrad, numbered at some 20,000 men, during its march from Anatolia to Syria by Turcomen and the *askari* of the Arslan clan warriors, near Dorylaeum, the scene of Bohemond's victory in 1098, was a trigger for knightly families in Germany, when they heard of the battle, and the martial prowess of the Turks, to forge genealogical tables and legends to give themselves Turkish-German origins. Heraldry began and developed rapidly during the early Crusades period, possibly as a response to increasingly full armour coverage, and the need to identify individuals on the battlefield, and in tournaments. Heraldic devices also acted as shorthand for complex family unions in the codices of knightly legitimacy.

The slaughter was so complete that it warranted only a short passage in Ibn al-Qalanasi's chronicle:

When the news of their approach became known and their purpose was bruited abroad, the governors of the neighbouring lands and of the Islamic territories in their proximity began to make preparations for warding them off and to muster their forces for engaging in the Holy War. They repaired to their outlets and mountainous defiles which hindered them from crossing

and debouching on the land of Islam, and assiduously launched raids upon their fringes. Death and slaughter commingled with the Franks until a vast number of them perished, and their suffering from lack of foodstuffs, forage and supplies, or the costliness of them if they were to be had at all, destroyed multitudes of them by hunger and disease. Fresh reports of their losses and of the destruction of their numbers were constantly arriving until the end of the year 542 [1148], with the result that men were restored to some degree of tranquillity of mind and began to gain some confidence in the failure of their enterprise, and their former distress and fear were alleviated.

The Anatolian Turks' destruction of the Franks was so rapid that they were unable to even gather together for defence. Nightfall gave respite and Conrad fled back to Byzantine-controlled Nicaea, but he had left almost his entire army on the killing field of Dorylaeum.

Details from Turkish Bows of the type that destroyed the armies of the Second Crusade, sixteenth-century examples

Christian warriors, He who gave His life for you, today demands yours in return. These are combats worthy of you, combats in which it is glorious to conquer and advantageous to die. Illustrious knights, generous defenders of the Cross, remember the example of your fathers, who conquered Jerusalem, and whose names are inscribed in Heaven. Abandon then the things that perish, to gather unfading palms and conquer a Kingdom that has no end . . .

Bernard of Clairvaux preaching the Second Crusade in Burgundy. 1146.

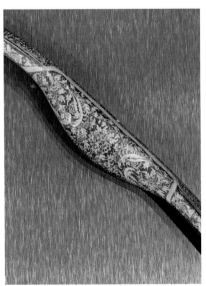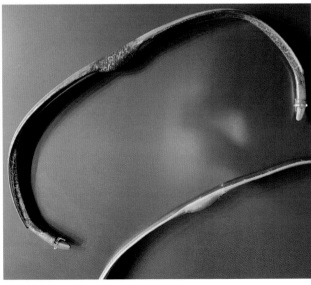

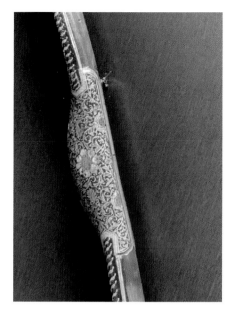
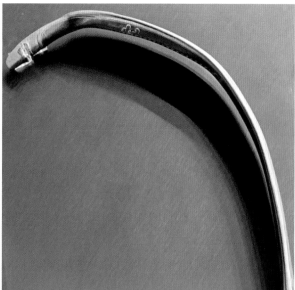

Conrad returned to Constantinople a sick man, but later embarked by ship for Palestine. Louis's army suffered a similar fate to that of the emperor's when the Turks cut off the army's main body from its vanguard and once more the Crusaders were routed by the sheer rapidity of the assault, and by the volume of shots delivered from the Turks' composite bows. Louis spent the night in a tree, surrounded by what was left of his bodyguard. He scraped together the remainder of his forces and marched to Byzantine territory. Louis sailed to Saint Symeon in March 1148, with only his household: his infantry attempted to march to Antioch and over half of them died en route.

At Antioch, Raymond attempted to swing Louis in favour of an attack on Aleppo but Louis rejected the plan and marched to Palestine. The Crusade was instead directed at Damascus. Many historians have suggested that the Crusaders remained secure from the risk of a united and belligerent Muslim Syria until this abortive campaign against Damascus, and that the Damascenes were effectively forced by the Franks' actions to abandon their policy of non-alignment. There is a degree of truth in this, but Nur al-Din had already shown that he was not averse to short-term coalitions with the Damascenes against the Crusaders, and he now had a marriage connection with the effective ruler of Damascus. Furthermore, Damascus did not actually succumb to the combination of charm and threat that Nur al-Din employed until six years after the Crusade's defeat.

In fact, the targeting of Damascus, despite the treaties that existed between it and Jerusalem, was not as foolish as hindsight makes it appear. Damascus was the closest, potentially belligerent Turkish-controlled city to Jerusalem. Egypt might have been a better choice – particularly given the Franks later attempts to take it with far weaker forces than they had available in 1148 – but Egypt was quiescent at this point, and the Turks, by virtue of their successes, had made themselves the prime threat to the Franks.

The real blunder was therefore not the choice of objective, but the execution of the plan to take it. The Crusaders arrived in the environs of Damascus on 24 July and immediately found themselves able to invest only a fraction of the long walls and that all the wells outside the city had been filled or poisoned. As they moved through the gardens outside the western wall, they were met by a furious

assault from *ghazis* but continued to advance and were able to use the trees of the orchards to begin building siege towers. For a short time it looked as if the city might fall and a desperate defence ensued at each corner or outcrop of the walls. William of Tyre tells us that:

> There were men with lances hiding inside of the walls. When these men saw our men passing by, they would stab them as they passed, through little peepholes in the walls which were cleverly designed for this purpose . . .

These men were paid for each head that they returned to Damascus with. They slowed the Crusaders whilst the forces that would finish their work assembled.

48 The Battle of Inab, by the fifteenth-century miniature painter Jean Colombe

> With the ingenuity which is characteristic of those suffering misery and adversity, they had recourse to desperate devices. In all the sections of the city which faced our camps they heaped up huge, tall beams, for they could only hope that while our men were working to tear down these barriers they might be able to flee in the opposite direction with their wives and children.
>
> William of Tyre, *Historia Rerum in Partibus Transmarinis Gestaru.*

Turcomen began to arrive in Damascus through the Aleppo and Baghdad gates, which had not been blockaded. They assembled on 25 July and made a dawn attack. They were held at a distance by the Crusaders' crossbowmen, but took the field again the next day. The orchards forced a dispersed battle on the two sides but the Turcoman troopers and infantry archers were supported by mangonels mounted on the city wall that destroyed the Crusaders' barricades with *naft*.

The Crusaders attempted to retire and lost many of their horses in their retreat, and then in desperation decided to move their entire attack against the south-eastern wall of the city. They knew that Nur al-Din and his brother were already marching from Aleppo and Mosul and would arrive within days. The planned assault never took place, however, as the army's morale was broken, and instead a retreat began.

Worse was to come. Louis and Conrad left Outremer with their troops in 1149 and Baldwin had lost the esteem of his vassals and now had neither the men nor the required prestige to ride to Antioch's aid when Raymond's army was virtually annihilated by Nur al-Din on 29 June at the Battle of Inab.

Raymond had managed to force Nur al-Din to raise a siege of the fortress of Inab, but had then been surrounded in his camp. The next morning Raymond charged the Turkish ring but arrows rained down from all sides and a Kurd, Shirkuh, of the same Ayyubid clan as the soldier who had saved Zangi's life, took Raymond's head. It was sent, like that of Raymond's father in-law, to the caliph in a silver box.

Joscelin was the next prince to suffer at Nur al-Din's hands as the north of Syria slipped away from Crusader control. He was captured while raiding Muslim lands and was blinded and imprisoned until his death ten years later.

Baldwin managed to secure the city of Antioch, and Joscelin's widow sold all her possessions beyond Antioch to the Byzantine Emperor, as Muslim raiding had made her position untenable. Baldwin arranged the evacuation of Latins from the region. Baldwin only had about 500 troops to cover this column of non-combatants as they marched from Tel Bashir to Antioch. Nur al-Din's troopers harassed the column almost at will and repeatedly cut off those marching at its rear. Baldwin, however, managed the task with exemplary skill and with his baggage train looking like a porcupine, such was the volume of arrows sticking out of it, he arrived safely in Antioch with the refugees.

Only one success can be claimed by the Second Crusade, and it had nothing to do with kings or emperors leading men to the Holy Sepulchre. On their way to the Holy Land Flemish, Norman, English, Scottish, and some German Crusaders, stopped off in Portugal. They tarried there, and helped the Portuguese in the capture of Lisbon in 1147.

49 Prester John in a Few of his Many Manifestations, from the nineteenth to the twentieth centuries

I will fetch you a tooth-picker now from the furthest inch of Asia,
bring you the length of Prester John's foot . . .

William Shakespeare, *Much Ado About Nothing*, Act II Scene I.

Prester John, the legendary Christian monarch and a descendant of the Three Magi, may have existed in the imaginations of Europeans before the Crusades, but the disasters of the Second Crusade, the rumours of Islam being defeated by some mighty ruler in the East and the hopes that this great warrior king would appear and save Outremer gave real life to the myth.

The Nestorian Christians had worked hard in the East to convert the peoples of Central Asia beyond the lands of Islam, and it was assumed that Prester John was a Nestorian patriarch, or that his people had been converted by Thomas the Apostle during the saint's travels through to India. The marvellous products that were now entering Europe via the Italian port cities fuelled the idea that Prester John ruled over lands full of riches.

Then in the 1150s stories started to reach the Crusader Kingdom of disasters striking the eastern lands of Islam. As we have seen above, the eastern part of the Saljuq Sultanate was embroiled in Transoxanian affairs from 1100 onwards, with continual incursions of Ghuzz Turks who were being pushed west by Turco-Mongolic 'federations' that whilst raiding China, existed in the steppe beyond the Middle Kingdom's borders. One of these, the Khitans, in fact took a Chinese dynastic name, the Liao, and ruled parts of northern China until they were displaced and pushed back into the steppe by the rise of the Jurchen of Manchuria who would go on to form the Jin Dynasty, the second of a succession of three alien dynasties that were to rule in China.

The Khitai remained a powerful force despite losing China, and their 'new' steppe-state displaced the Ghuzz Turks, who having nowhere else to go started to enter the Dar al-Islam once again en

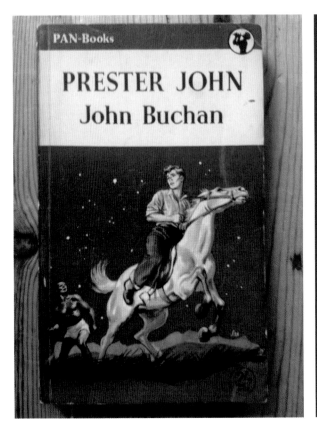

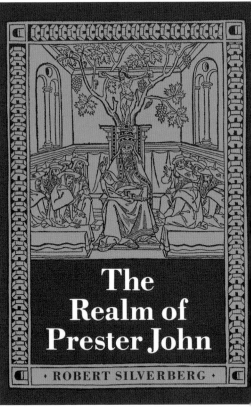

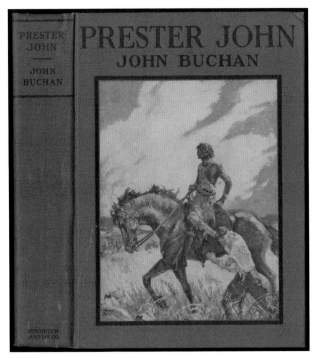

masse. The Sultanate's panicked response to this 'tsunami' of people was to go to war with the Khitans but the unfortunate Sultan Sanjar was totally defeated by them in 1141 at the Battle of the Qatwan Steppe. The great Saljuq Sultanate was already perhaps in its death throes but then the further defeat of the sultan by the Ghuzz Turks in 1153 essentially finished the state.

The lords of Outremer might have been cheered by the tales heard from merchants of these victories for Prester John, but they also realised that with Nur al-Din coming close to uniting all of Muslim Syria against them they needed to look to themselves to save their kingdom, and to some way of changing the rules of the game. They began to see Egypt as a new promised land.

⑤⓪ The *Douane, Dogana,* and Customs Post, an idea, for good or ill, taken from the *Diwan* of the Arabs to Europe and beyond during the Crusades

When death with claw-like nails strikes at her prey, no amulet avails . . .

Ibn al-Qalanasi, *The Chronicle of Damascus.*

Baldwin III died in February 1162. Despite the difficult start to his reign and the increasingly frequent blows that Nur al-Din inflicted upon the king's lands, Baldwin had achieved a good deal considering the poor hand he had been dealt by fate. Ascalon had finally fallen to the Crusaders. This frightened Damascus enough to maintain its non-aggression pact with the Franks, and gave the entire

DOUANES & DROITS INDIRECTS

maritime trade of Syria over to Frankish control. The Arabic *diwan* tariffs, soon to be copied as the *douane* and *dogana* in France and Italy, and eventually to become what we understand today as customs dues, maintained the coffers of the kingdom and helped to pay local infantry, turcopoles and mercenaries. Ascalon was also a stepping stone on the road to Egypt, and Egypt would soon become the chief strategic focus for the Crusaders and Nur al-Din.

Nur al-Din had finally brought Damascus under his control, and the city's wealth paid for his burgeoning army. It fell to him in a relatively straightforward way. His Aleppan forces had chased the Damascene *askari* back to the gate leading to the city's Jewish quarter. Then an elderly Jewish lady lowered a rope to one of the foot soldiers below. Nur al-Din's standard went up on the wall and a woodcutter followed the old lady's example by smashing the lock of the East Gate and allowing the Aleppans easy entry. A united Syria was called into existence and its new sultan granted Jerusalem a one-year truce, in complete contradiction to his recent jihad propaganda. He needed to attend to the north of Syria where the

Byzantines were again stirring up trouble, but all military activity from both sides was then cut short by a series of earthquakes in 1156.

Nur al-Din returned to the south to push the Franks from Banyas. He captured many knights and they were paraded through Damascus on camels, each with his banner attached so the crowds could recognise them, but this campaign was also cut short by continuing earth tremors. Then in 1157 Kilij Arslan II, the Sultan of Iconium, threatened Antioch. Nur al-Din immediately entered into a truce with Baldwin to allow Jerusalem to support Antioch. The jihad was put on hold as Nur al-Din considered Antioch as a soon to be acquired possession of the Zangid clan. In August, Nur al-Din set out with a large force that arrayed itself before Antioch and essentially created an exclusion zone around the city, through which neither the Franks nor the Turks of Anatolia could pass.

The sultan fell seriously ill in October 1157 but his lieutenants kept Syria under control. But he had to return to the field in 1158, despite ongoing poor health, as the Crusaders raided around Damascus. In 1159 the action moved again to the north as the Byzantines secured suzerainty over several Anatolian Turkish lords and these distractions meant stalemate in the south. Both the Crusaders and the Zangids looked to the ailing Fatimid state and its treasure to support their campaigns, the contest for Egypt would be between Nur al-Din and Amalric, who succeeded his childless brother in February 1162.

Monarchie Franque et Monarchie Musulman L'equilibre

51 Al-Azhar Mosque, Cairo, c. 970

My uncle then said to Nur al-Din. 'It is absolutely necessary that Yusuf go with me'. And Nur al-Din thus repeated his orders. I tried to explain the state of financial embarrassment in which I found myself. He ordered that money be given to me and I had to go, like a man being led off to his death.

The later sultan, Saladin, reflecting on the campaign
in Egypt against Amalric in the 1160s.

Egypt had fallen very far from the glory days of the al-Azhar mosque's construction in 970. As perhaps the first university in the world its *raison d'être* of propagating the Fatimid creed was pretty much at an end

too by the 1160s, as the dynasty was now paying tribute to the Franks just in order to stave off invasion. It had run through fifteen different *wazirs*. Every one of them had been involved in deadly standoffs with the caliphs, and only one of them had survived his tenure. Cliques of officers that backed different candidates for the *wazirate* broke the state apart. It was unfortunate for Amalric that Shawar, one of the losers in the deadly competition for the office, fled not to him, but to Nur al-Din's court to seek aid against his successor. Amalric invaded Egypt in September 1163 to pre-empt any move by the Muslims and got to Bilbays after defeating a force sent against him by the new *wazir*, Dirgham. His hopes were then, however, literally washed away when the Nile dykes were broken open by the Egyptians and his army's camp was flooded. A hasty retreat from the mud of the delta back to Palestine soon followed.

In Damascus, Nur al-Din hurried to organise a response to Amalric's grab for Egypt, and Shawar enthusiastically told the sultan that all expenses for the expedition could be met from the Egyptian treasury. Nur al-Din selected the trusty Shirkuh to lead the mission, which was certainly wise as an abundance of cunning and durability would be needed for the campaign. He then made a diversionary attack on northern Palestine in April 1164 to allow Shirkuh and his nephew Saladin, along with a small force, a window of opportunity in which to return Shawar to the *wazir*'s palace. They took a long route east of the Jordan to the Red Sea before riding across the Sinai to Bilbays, and were at the walls of Cairo by 1 May. Shirkuh's sudden appearance seems to have paralysed Dirgham, and the city fell bloodlessly. Shawar was put back in office whilst the body of Dirgham was left to rot in the streets. Shawar then rapidly double-crossed Shirkuh, and in July 1164 Almaric marched on Egypt again, this time at the invitation of the *wazir*. Shirkuh abandoned his barracks at Cairo, and held the Crusaders in newly-prepared positions at Bilbays, but the situation looked hopeless unless something could be done to pull Amalric away from Egypt.

Nur al-Din struck at Harim, defeated a coalition of Crusader, Armenian and Byzantine forces and captured Bohemond III of Antioch. Amalric was forced to negotiate for a mutual withdrawal of forces, and both armies left Egypt in October 1164. Amalric went straight to Antioch to defend the city. He managed to secure the situation there, but then had to march south, as his own territory was now under attack by Nur al-Din. In fact, things were going so well for Nur al-Din in Syria that he did not hazard for Egypt again until he was provoked by Shawar.

52 The City of Alexandria

Vidi quel Bruto che cacciò Tarquino,
Lucrezia, Iulia, Marzïa e Corniglia;
e solo, in parte, vidi 'l Saladino.

I saw that Brutus who expelled Tarquin,
Lucretia, Julia, Marcia, and Cornelia,
and I saw Saladin, by himself, apart.

Dante, *L'inferno*, Canto IV, 127–129.

Shawar secured a treaty of mutual assistance with Amalric and Nur al-Din responded with another expedition led by Shirkuh and Saladin in early 1167. Shirkuh slipped past the Crusaders and got his

men between Cairo and Amalric's advancing troops, then as the Crusaders crossed the Nile he fled up the river valley. Amalric set off in pursuit with only his knights, as his infantry could not keep up with the pace of Shirkuh's retreat. The Battle of al-Babayn was fought on the fringes of the desert where soft sand and the steep slopes of the dunes made the Crusader charge of limited value. Amalric made

a charge at Shirkuh's centre with a contingent of his knights, but the troops positioned there under the command of Saladin quickly retreated. Amalric then found himself under an archery assault from two charging wings and also cut off from the rest of his forces. He managed to cut his way out of the mass of injured and dying knights that his force had become, and returned to his main force. He rallied as many men as he could around his standard, formed them into a close-order column, cleared the field, and headed back to Cairo.

Shirkuh then raced to Alexandria, which was on the point of rebellion against Shawar, and Amalric responded by besieging the city with the support of a Pisan fleet. Within a month the city was starving. Shirkuh broke out under cover of night from the city, leaving Saladin in charge of the remaining men, and attempted to foment rebellion against Shawar in Upper Egypt. Nur al-Din brought war to Amalric's lands again and the king was forced to negotiate. Saladin was held as a hostage during the talks, and he became friendly with the Crusader Humphrey of Toron. The Syrian army was allowed to leave Egypt unmolested and Amalric left soon after in August. He had secured an increased tribute to Jerusalem and the right to have troops and a military attaché garrisoned in Cairo.

Amalric's demands on the Egyptians for tribute required huge tax increases. This, coupled with the presence of *Franj* troops in Cairo, ate away at Shawar's support. A Crusader army led by Count William of Nevers also arrived in Palestine in the summer of 1168, and this seems to have set Amalric's mind that Egypt should be reduced before it rebelled against his puppet.

Shawar opened protracted negotiations with the king, and sent to Nur al-Din once again for aid. Cairo's defenders set fires in the old city that blazed for 50 days, in order to deny the Crusaders its markets and shelter. Shirkuh and Saladin returned once more, but this time with an army larger than Amalric's. The Crusader siege was falling apart as 'camp-sickness' took hold and the king took his army out of Egypt on 2 January 1169.

Shirkuh took the position of *wazir* with the support of the Fatimid Caliph and executed Shawar. Shirkuh did not, however, enjoy the pleasures of the office too long, as he died in his bath in March 1169.

53 A Polo Game: an Illustration from the Divan of Mir 'Alishir Nava'l, Iran, sixteenth century

Religion is in darkness because of the absence of his light
The age is in grief because of the loss of its commander.
Let Islam mourn the defender of its people
And Syria mourn the protector of its kingdom and its borders

Abu Shama, a contemporary poet, mourning Nur al-Din.

Nur al-Din died on 15 May 1174 following a heart attack brought on by a polo match. He had always been a gifted and aggressive player of the game, much as he had been a gifted politician and an aggressive military leader. Indeed the two almost went hand-in-hand in the Turkish world as polo had come with them from Central Asia during the great migrations, and, like the great hunts, it was a 'bloodless drill' that taught many of the skills required on the battlefield.

He was about 60 when he died and he was rightly remembered by the populace of Muslim Syria as the man who had taken away the very real fear that the *Franj* would conquer Aleppo and Damascus. The last years of his reign were a success but were marred by constant and mutual suspicion between him and his lieutenant in Egypt, Saladin. Nur al-Din made constant demands on the Egyptian treasury and Egyptian army that Saladin would not, or could not, comply with. Indeed it might even be suggested that Saladin viewed the Crusader state as a shield protecting his new acquisition from the sultan, and also recognised what a dangerous game he was playing.

In fairness to Saladin he was *wazir* to a Shiite-Ismaili caliph and had only a small body of Syrian troopers to counter the still large, if virtually unmanageable, forces of the Fatimid army. He quickly seized lands and properties from senior Fatimid emirs, and used the funds and property he garnered from this to buy the services and loyalties of the Turkish Mamluks of the Fatimid army. By these actions he tied Syrian and Egyptian troops to his personal fortunes. He pushed the black troops of the Fatimid army, some 30,000 men, into a revolt because of his, possibly intentional, indifference to their welfare during the summer of 1169, but their leader's attempts to bring Amalric to their aid failed, as his messenger, dressed in peasant rags, failed to slip by Saladin's Turkish guards who noticed his fancy palace slippers.

Saladin had gambled but he knew that he had bought enough loyalty among the Turkish cavalry to crush the Sudanese troops. The Africans attempted a coup, but Saladin's troops burnt their lodgings to the ground and slaughtered their families. Those that survived fled to Gaza but Turanshah, Saladin's oldest brother, decimated them.

By 1174 Nur al-Din was becoming convinced that his lieutenant was becoming too strong and that Egypt's tax revenues, needed for the Syrian jihad, were being salted away by Saladin. Nur al-Din sent an inspector to Egypt to check the tax remittances and the inspector duly submitted a fairly damning report to the sultan. Mosul and Aleppo were immediately abuzz with rumours that Nur al-Din was mustering his forces for an attack on Egypt. It was said later that 'Fortune Made a King' when Saladin became Sultan of both Syria and Egypt. He was perhaps fortunate indeed that Nur al-Din died before the attack could be made.

54 Yemen, Saladin's bolthole, should all his plans come to nothing

O Allah bestow your blessings on our Medina, and bestow your blessings on our Mecca, and bestow your blessings on our Sham, and bestow your blessings on our Yemen.

From the Hadith of Najd.

Saladin and Nur al-Din had attempted joint campaigns in 1171 and 1173, when Saladin attacked Karak and Shawbak, the two great Crusader fortresses in the Transjordan, but in both ventures the two armies failed to join up.

The Crusaders had suffered the same issue of co-ordination in their attempts to take Egypt from the sea with the assistance of Byzantium in 1169, though in truth much of this was related to avarice over the expected spoils of the venture. The emperor dispatched a fleet of 230 ships and Amalric was to march before the end of the campaign season, but fortunately for Saladin the allies wrangled over treasure and over tactics, as the Franks insisted on marching to the Nile Delta rather than being carried by Byzantine transports. This may have been wise, however, as when the Byzantine fleet arrived at the port of Damietta they found their way barred by a giant chain. A siege was begun at the end

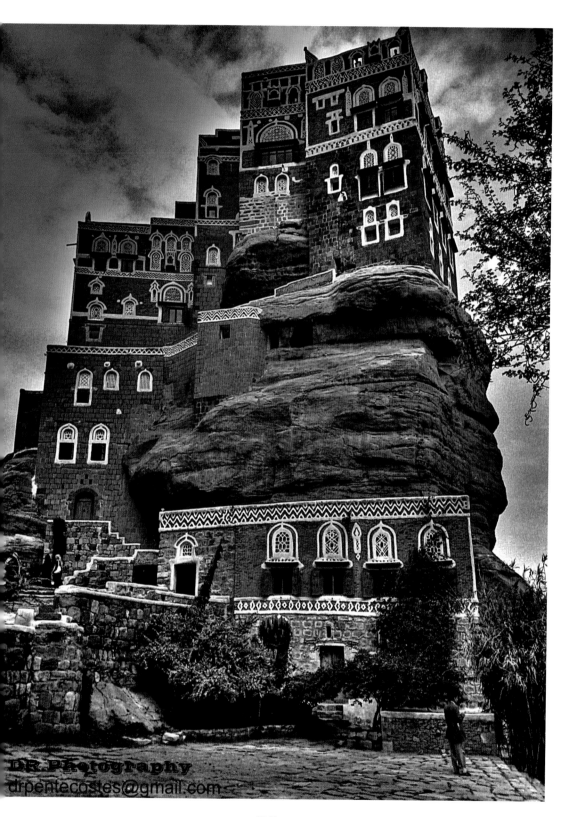

of October and there was still some hope of success, as the African troops were in full revolt, but Damietta resisted all assaults.

Then the weather turned and rains destroyed the Franks' morale and the ensuing mud made movement almost impossible. They withdrew after 35 days and a severe storm destroyed half the Byzantine fleet during its return to Constantinople.

Saladin took the Crusader fortress-city of Ayla at the head of the Persian Gulf, near modern-day Aqaba, in 1170. The venture required the dismantling of ships and their transport across the Sinai to the Red Sea, where they joined the assault on the port. These raids may have been aimed at showing Saladin's loyalty to Nur al-Din, as tensions were rising between the two men.

Throughout 1171 Nur al-Din pressured Saladin to finish the Fatimid line and impose Sunnism. Saladin's more admiring biographers claim that he could not bring himself to kill the sickly young caliph, but his hand was forced by a citizen of Mosul who was visiting Cairo. This gentleman, who was apparently very wealthy, entered the Friday mosque, climbed the pulpit ahead of the regular Ismaili preacher, and said the *khutba* in the name of the Abbasid caliph. There was no protest from the congregation and absolute quietude on the streets. The gentleman's largesse may have had something to do with the way that the Fatimid dynasty died so quietly, and almost without grieving on the part of its citizens. Its last caliph died, in his sleep, only a few days later and the women and men of the ruling house who survived him were separated so that the line, which claimed descent from the Prophet Muhammad's daughter, might die out naturally.

Egypt belonged once more to the Sunni world and a diploma of rule was sure to come to Nur al-Din sooner or later. As we have seen Saladin was hot and cold in his support of the sultan. In February 1174 he sent his brother to Yemen to clear it of Fatimid supporters and to secure it as a possible sanctuary for the Ayyubid family should he should fail in his dangerous balancing act.

55 Saladin remains a potent icon for unity and resistance in the Arab world, despite the Sultan being a Kurd. This movie poster advertises, *The Search for Saladin*

If our late Sultan had detected among you a man as worthy of his confidence as me, would he not have entrusted him with the leadership of Egypt, the most important of his provinces? You may be sure that had Nur al-Din not died so soon he would have designated me to educate his son and to watch over him.
The Kurd, Saladin, making his intention to take on the role of *atabeg* to Nur al-Din's heir very clear to the Turkish emirs of Syria.

Al-Salih, the son of Nur al-Din, was still a child when his father died. With the regency of al-Salih came power and Saladin attempted early on to secure his right to act as the child's *atabeg*. Nur al-Din's state also began to fracture, starting with Mosul, and then Gumushtigin, Nur al-Din's chief eunuch, took al-Salih to Aleppo and declared himself to be the boy's protector.

THE CRUSADES IN 100 OBJECTS

Saladin's propagandists responded with a message that those who chose to join him in his mission of defeating the Crusaders were 'in one valley and those who think ill of us are in another'. It did not work, and the Syrian emirs concluded a truce with Amalric, but then the king died in July 1174 of dysentery before the anti-Egypt alliance was fully consolidated, and the Zangid emirs fled from Damascus for fear of the ruler of Egypt. Saladin took only 700 men with him to Damascus and its gates were opened to him by members of his clan, the Ayyubids. Saladin was free from interference from the Crusaders as Amalric's son, Baldwin IV, was only a 13-year-old minor, and a leper. Factions formed in Outremer over the succession to this boy-king, who was expected to be a weak, short-lived monarch who would not sire an heir. Jerusalem was politically paralysed and the kingdom's later fatal divisions began with Baldwin IV's accession.

Saladin intended to prosecute the jihad but had first to bring Syria fully under his control, and his war against the Zangids was carried out under the pretence of carrying out his legal duties of guardianship of al-Salih. In fact, he did not move to occupy Aleppo until after the death of al-Salih in 1181. Saladin's intervention also averted a destructive internecine war amongst the petty princes, and after September 1176, with his marriage to Nur al-Din's widow, Khatun, and his obvious pre-eminence among the emirs, it also followed accepted custom.

Saladin's main aim in the years between 1174 and 1186 was to build an army and an alliance capable of taking on the grinding war that pushing the Crusader Kingdom into the sea would require. He was also, unlike his mentor Shirkuh, a cautious general. He rarely gambled and always looked to have superior numbers in any engagement. Battle is always a risky venture and Saladin was keen to pursue it only if the odds were stacked absolutely in his favour. In desperation at Saladin's gobbling-up of cities and land, Gumushtigin responded with what we would call today asymmetrical warfare. He persuaded Syria's Ismaili Assassin grand master, Sinan, to make an attempt on Saladin's life. The Ismaili Assassins had struggled to survive in Syria during Nur al-Din's reign, but in the confused political landscape of the 1170s they bid once more for political power in northern Syria. Assassins, disguised as soldiers in Saladin's army, tried to gain access to the sultan's tent, but they were challenged by an emir. They stabbed the emir and one Assassin got into the tent, only to have his head slashed off by a guard's scimitar. More Assassins then forced their way into the tent, but Saladin's bodyguards killed them to a man. It would not be the last time that the Assassins and the sultan would clash.

Fortune Makes a King

56 The Hakawati, a Traditional Syrian Teller of Arabic Stories and Reciter of Legends

Again and again we were on the verge of destruction, nor would God have delivered us if it were not for some future duty.

The Sultan Saladin looking back on the dangers of the 1170s.

Saladin has been well served by his contemporary Arabic biographers, and by Western troubadours, poets and historians. Stories about the great sultan who retook Jerusalem from the *Franj*, and who died with only one gold and forty-seven silver coins as his personal fortune, were still being told by *hakawati* in the twenty-first century in teahouses and coffee shops across Syria. It is easy to understand why. Whilst Saladin was decidedly a man of war, and was intolerant of religious unorthodoxy to the extent of crucifying unbelievers, freethinkers and heretics, he is also the one individual of the Crusades period who clearly shows a nature inclined towards clemency, concern for the population and chivalry, and his occasional lapses into brutality might be excused by the need to survive and prosper in the cut-throat world of twelfth-century Syrian politics, and by the fanatical nature of his Christian adversaries.

The sultan was a formidable enemy once roused and on 13 April 1175, he crushed the combined forces of Mosul and Aleppo at the Battle of the Horns of Hama, near the River Orontes. One cavalry charge was enough to clear the field of the Aleppan *askari*, and the baggage train and the infantry were both abandoned to their fate. The Mosul contingent was particularly badly, but courageously, led. Saladin said of its leader, Izz al-Din, that he was, 'either the bravest man present on the field that day or a complete fool'.

Saladin was now in undisputed possession of Damascus and a large part of northern Syria, with virtual suzerainty over Aleppo. However, he failed to achieve full caliphal recognition of his rights in northern Syria, despite sending envoys to Baghdad in the summer of 1175 and such a recognition was vital for him to be able to claim unchallenged leadership in the Holy War. The rise of Saladin the Kurd, in a theatre dominated by Turks for over a hundred years, may have played badly in Saljuq Baghdad, but then enemies were also to be found closer to home too. In May 1176, as Saladin was resting alone in the tent of one of his emirs, an Ismaili Assassin rushed in and struck at him with a dagger. He was only saved by the close-fitting mail coif that covered his head and neck. The Assassin then slashed at his throat, but Saladin, who was a small but extremely powerful man, struck at his attacker's arm and slapped the blow away. One of Saladin's emirs heard the commotion and rushed into the tent and the Assassin was overpowered and killed. Then another Ismaili burst into the tent and attacked the sultan. Fortunately, the guard had now arrived and the Assassin was hacked to pieces. When the Assassins' bodies were examined it was found that they were both members of Saladin's close personal bodyguard.

57 The Assassin Castle of Maysaf in Syria, twelfth century

Do you threaten a duck with the river? Prepare means for disaster and don a garment against catastrophe; for I will defeat you from within your own ranks and take vengeance against you at your own place, and you will be as one who encompasses his own destruction . . .

The Syrian Grand Master, Sinan, mocking Saladin's threats against the Assassin *fidai*, a cult dedicated to a love of sacrificial death.

Saladin besieged the forbidding Ismaili Assassin castle of Masyaf in August 1176. He was riding through a forest with his bodyguard towards the fortress when an Assassin dropped from a tree to try once more to murder him. Fortunately for Saladin, the Assassin's timing was off and he landed on the

rump of the sultan's horse, fell backwards to the ground, and was trampled and hacked to death by the bodyguard riding close behind. Saladin then had a tall wooden tower built, in which he would sleep at night, and was never seen without mail during the day.

Saladin then rapidly came to terms with the Assassins after threats were made against every member of the Ayyubid ruling family, and after it was made very clear to the sultan just how many of his own Mamluks were members of the creed. An agreement was struck which ensured the safety of the Assassins' enclaves from the sultan's army and allowed Saladin to continue with the prosecution of his campaign against Aleppo and indeed gave him the opportunity to employ Assassins for his own political ends. He almost certainly used them against the house of Zangi soon after, but his secret relationship with Sinan would bring its greatest benefit to him at the end of his reign.

Saladin indulged in some uncharacteristic adventurism by raiding in Gaza and pursuing the apparently retreating army of Baldwin IV to Ascalon. The sultan then made a plundering raid around Jaffa and Ramla. Baldwin IV, with a dogged dedication to duty and to defence that characterised his wise approach to war, followed at a distance. Then, near Ramla, at Mont Gisard, he struck at Saladin's *askari*, which he knew would be the rallying point for the army once they realised that they were under attack. The Mamluks were thrown into complete confusion by the Crusaders' charge and the panic spread. Huge casualties were taken by every part of the Muslim army, which was impeded from forming up to mount a response by baggage animals and cattle they had looted from the Franks. This plunder was all lost and Baldwin IV pursued Saladin until nightfall. The retreat to Egypt hardly went any better; it was undertaken in heavy rain and under constant attack by Bedouins. It was the heaviest loss in battle that Saladin would ever endure and he learnt much from the debacle.

The disaster of Mont Gisard also kept Saladin from taking the field in 1178 and he spent the year building up his navy and restoring his army's strength. He started a trend that would continue through the later Ayyubids, of an increasing reliance on Mamluk Turks who, almost exclusively, hailed from the Caucasus. These men would eventually take the sultanate of Egypt from the Ayyubids, defeat the Mongols and crush the Crusader Kingdom.

58 Devalued Dinars: Crusader and Arabic coinage of the twelfth century, Iraqi banknotes of the twenty-first century

To say the name of a pure gold dinar was like mentioning the name of a wife to a jealous husband, while to get such a coin in one's hand was like crossing the doors of paradise ...

Al-Maqrizi on the currency crisis in Egypt and Syria in the late twelfth century.

By the time that Saladin faced the Third Crusade he had nearly exhausted both the Syrian and Egyptian treasuries. As early as 1171 he had devalued Egypt's currency to meet the costs of its defence. This was reckoned as 'a calamity in Egypt, because gold and silver left Egypt, not to return again'.

However, Saladin was not entirely to blame for the lack of trust placed by merchants and citizens in Egypt's currency. Gold coins struck by the Crusaders throughout the eleventh and twelfth centuries copied Arabic dinars, and their introduction into the monetary system of

the eastern Mediterranean was one of the earliest, albeit accidental, instances of economic warfare. The Arabic dinar was so untrusted by the fourteenth century that an alternative for international trade was looked for by merchants and found in the 'new' gold ducats of the Italian maritime republics. An important element of the control of trade therefore moved from the East to the West during the Crusades. As we will see, later, when the 'blue ocean' expeditions of the Spanish brought vast quantities of silver to Europe, similar damage would be done to the silver coin-based economy of the Turks.

By the close of the 1170s Saladin was draining the treasury to build up the Egyptian navy and to support his Syrian possessions through a vicious famine. Baldwin IV and his state were suffering too, and in April 1179 the opportunity to raid cattle from the Crusader castle of Belfort was irresistible. Saladin's nephew trailed the Crusaders with part of his *askari*, and lit beacons to show their progress so that Saladin could intercept them with a larger force. The Crusaders were surprised by the Muslims, who were hidden in the narrow rocky valleys of the area. They emerged in small groups at the gallop and assaulted the disorganised Franks with showers of arrows. The Crusaders retreated in disarray and Humphrey of Toron, Saladin's friend since he was held as a hostage during Shirkuh's campaigns in Egypt, was killed whilst protecting Baldwin IV from the rain of arrows that was falling all around them.

Saladin then began to raid Crusader farmland using starving Bedouin as a vanguard, backed by heavy cavalry. Baldwin responded consistently to protect his subjects, but his strategy came undone at the Marj Ayyun or 'Field of Springs'. His troops were caught between Saladin's force arriving from the east and from the north. Saladin went on to besiege, storm and destroy the fortress of Chastellet at Jacob's Ford, on the upper Jordan.

Back in 1178, Saladin had offered 100,000 dinars (of presumably dubious quality) to the Franks if they agreed to cease their building but they had refused. With Chastellet's destruction the whole frontier of the Kingdom of Jerusalem was now virtually uninhabitable for the Franks, and the kingdom lay open to Saladin's armies.

59 The city of Jeddah. Its merchants' houses reflected the city's wealth and the fact that it was, and is, the gateway to Islam's holiest cities

The hour of one's death is not brought nearer by exposing oneself to danger nor delayed by being overcautious . . .
The twelfth-century soldier Usama Ibn Munqidh, on fate and God's will.

Byzantium had been crippled by the disaster of the Battle of Myriokephalon in September 1176 during the Empire's final, unsuccessful attempt to recover the interior of Anatolia and 1180 saw the conclusion of a truce between Saladin and the new Byzantine emperor, Alexius II. Alexius was in fact the puppet of Andronicus Comnenus, and he initiated his reign with a massacre of Latins in Constantinople.

In August 1182 Saladin attempted a combined land and sea siege of Beirut. Possession of a port on the coast was vital to the retaking of Syria and the conquest of Beirut would severely hamper communications between the northern and southern states of Outremer. Thirty galleys were committed to the siege, but Saladin's land forces retired after the failure of an amphibious landing and the arrival of thirty-three Latin galleys. The sultan had failed but it was obvious to the Crusaders that they were being boxed in. It may have been this that decided Reynald of Châtillon, the lord of Karak, to move from targeting caravans that travelled between Syria and Arabia to launching a flotilla of vessels on the Red Sea. He besieged Ayla, and he sank sixteen Muslim vessels and captured two more. The Muslim chroniclers tell us that he wanted to strike at Mecca via Jeddah. He was defeated in his ambitions by the Egyptian fleet, as ships were taken overland from Cairo and launched in the Red Sea.

Saladin wrote to the caliph complaining that while he had been defending Jeddah, Medina and Mecca, Aleppo remained rebellious against the leader of the jihad. The city, however, finally fell to him in 1183, after some deft negotiation with the Sultan Kilij Arslan II, which isolated it from all Anatolian Turcoman support, and some highly adept propaganda that linked the submission of its only source of succour, Mosul, to the greater project of expelling the Franks from the Holy Land:

> *This little Jazira is the lever which will set in motion the great Jazira; it is the point of division and centre of resistance, and once it is set in its place in the chain of alliances, the whole armed might of Islam will be co-ordinated to engage the forces of unbelief . . .*

All around Aleppo Turkish emirs began to come to Saladin to proclaim their loyalty and soon the city was bereft of allies. Saladin invested it on 21 May 1183 but was reluctant to fight the old guard of Nur al-Din. He attempted to woo them with fine words about how they were, 'the soldiers of the jihad, who had in the past done great services for Islam . . . whose gallantry and courage had gained his admiration'. The *Nuriya* were, however, determined to have their day of battle and the sultan was unable to restrain his Mamluks, who wanted to show that they were the new *corps d'élite*. Saladin's brother, Taj al-Muluk, was killed in a fierce clash between the two sides, but this did at least finally bring the two sides to the negotiating table. The sultan completed his work in the north, by concluding a peace treaty and Muslim prisoner release with Bohemond III of Antioch, and then he went to war with Jerusalem.

 ## Poster for the Movie *Saladin and the Crusaders*, 1963. Often seen as a celebration of Colonel Nasser of Egypt, who wished, and failed, to replicate the Sultan's deeds

> *When we enter the enemy's terrain this is our army's battle order, our method of advancing and retreating, the position of our battalions, the place where our knights rise up, where our lances are to fall, the paths by which to direct our horses, the arenas for our coursers, the gardens for our roses, the site of our vicissitudes, the outlets of our desires, the scene on which we shall be transfigured . . .*
> Saladin addressing his army before they entered the lands of the Crusaders.

Jerusalem was ill-prepared for a contest. Raymond of Tripoli had been made regent, since Baldwin had gone into a terminal decline, but a faction under Baldwin's brother in-law, Guy of Lusignan, was contesting this control and accusing Raymond of plotting against the kingdom. The army of Jerusalem did not challenge Saladin when he raided Palestine, and appeared paralysed. Guy had managed to get himself named as regent over Raymond just before the sultan's incursions, but his failure to ride out, as Baldwin would have, lost him the regency. This humiliation would later lead him to a catastrophic error of judgement.

Raymond of Tripoli secured a truce with Saladin in early 1185, as Baldwin IV lay dying. Saladin also came close to death from a contagion that spread through his camp as he besieged Mosul. Despite extreme ill-health Saladin kept his troops at the walls. Then, following a visit from a delegation of Zangid princesses, Saladin agreed to negotiate. Mosul accepted his suzerainty in March 1186; the grand coalition was now finally complete and Outremer was in dire peril. The new king, Guy of Lusignan, was

not the man to save a kingdom. Raymond of Tripoli was forced to seek a further treaty with Saladin, this time for his own lands as his own king was mustering troops to attack Raymond's capital, Tiberias.

Saladin responded to Reynald of Châtillon's continuing attacks on Muslim caravans by sending his son, al-Afdal, to raid Palestine. He was met in battle by a rather foolhardy contingent of Templars and Hospitallers, who had ignored Raymond of Tripoli's advice to avoid conflict with the superior Muslim forces. They were caught by al-Afdal's troopers at Saffuriyah on 1 May and annihilated. The Master of the Hospital died with his men.

Saladin reviewed the army in May 1187. He now commanded about 12,000 regular troopers and the chroniclers indicate that a significant number of volunteer fighters or Mujahideen, auxiliaries and Turcomen were also attracted to his standard. The entire force probably numbered about 20,000 men. On 2 July Saladin began a siege of Tiberias and quickly took the lower town. The army of Jerusalem lay not far off at Saffuriyah, as it had been shadowing the Muslim army's progress. Guy had also called upon mercenaries and knights from Antioch to rally to him. Raymond warned Guy not to engage Saladin, but in truth the king's army was roughly equal in size to the sultan's and Guy still had the haunting memory of 1183 and his loss of the regency to spur him into action.

In truth, defeat would have been far more catastrophic for Saladin than for Guy. As at Mont Gisard, Saladin would have had to make a hazardous and protracted retreat. The Crusaders had been defeated many times before, but their army had always been preserved and the Muslims had been denied a decisive victory by the proximity of a fortified refuge. Saladin's greatest achievement of the campaign of 1187 was to trap the Christian army away from any sources of security, in exposed country, where a liquidation of the flower of Jerusalem's chivalry could be achieved.

Rose Petals in al-Quds

61 A Reliquary holding a piece of the True Cross. Twelfth century

When the ranks were drawn up and the arms distributed he made gifts of warhorses and scattered largesse, devoted himself to making donations and giving coveted prizes . . . distributed bundles of arrows, of which the soldiers received more than a quiverful. He made chargers gallop and brought forth an ample harvest of troops.

Imad al-Din at his hyperbolic best on Saladin's preparations before the Battle of the Horns of Hattin.

The Crusader army marched to the relief of Tiberias. They knew that they would be passing through arid country without water sources, but were headed for Lake Tiberias, where they could restock and rest before attempting to break the siege. They never made it there, because Saladin used the tactics that had often brought victory in the past to their optimum effect. His Turks and Kurds harassed and harried the Crusader column with fast attacks and volleys of arrows, with the consistent aim of breaking up the Crusaders' marching order and detaching their rearguard. Eventually, the Templars at the rear of the column could no longer sustain a defence against Saladin's troopers while continuing with the march. It was also impossible for the infantry, who were suffering particularly badly in the summer heat, to up the pace of the march

to escape the attentions of the raiders. Saladin's men forced the Franks to a halt and the Crusaders could now see that their route to Tiberias was blocked by the sultan's army. They made camp on a low hillside named the Horns of Hattin. In the Muslim camp, extra arrows were distributed to the men.

The next morning dawned with the *Franj* in a fearful condition. They were almost mad with thirst and any will to fight had been nearly extinguished by the gruelling march the day before. That said, the battle raged furiously, with both sides putting up a tenacious resistance. Muslim archers sent up clouds of arrows like thick swarms of locusts, and the Crusaders tried to fight their way toward Tiberias in the hope of reaching water. Saladin planted himself and his army in the way. He rode up and down the Muslim lines encouraging and restraining his troops where necessary. The Muslims then charged their enemy and almost broke through. Raymond of Tripoli made a charge, but only to bring his followers out of the battle as the Muslims set fire to the dry grass that covered the ground, and the Crusaders now had to endure smoke and flames, in addition to thirst, the summer heat, and the Muslim archery. Guy organised a series of charges, but each wave only diminished his numbers. He retreated up the hill and pitched his tent as a rallying point, the True Cross was captured but the king and 500 knights fought on.

Al-Malik al-Afdal, Saladin's son, wrote of a Crusader charge that forced the Muslims back. His father became distraught and tugged at his beard as he went forward crying, 'Away with the devil's lie!' Then the Muslims counter-attacked and drove the king back up the hill.

Al-Malik cried out, 'We have conquered them!' But then another courageous charge came that beat the Muslims back. Saladin urged his men back to the fight and Guy had to retreat once more.

Saladin's son cried out again, 'We have beaten them!' His father turned and said, 'Be quiet, we shall not have beaten them until the tent falls!' As he spoke the tent fell and Saladin dismounted and prostrated himself in thanks to God, weeping for joy.

62 A Statue of Saladin celebrating the Sultan's victory at the Horns of Hattin, Damascus, inaugurated in 1993

With him was a whole band of scholars and sufis and a certain number of devout men and ascetics; each begged to be allowed to kill one of them and drew his sword and rolled back his sleeve. Saladin, his face joyful, was sitting on his dais; the unbelievers in black despair . . . there were some who slashed and cut cleanly, and were thanked for it; some who refused and failed to act, and others took their places . . .

Imad al-Din writing of Saladin's wrath upon the Templars and Hospitallers after the Battle of the Horns of Hattin.

Guy, Reynald and an exhausted group of Templars and Hospitallers lay prostrate from exhaustion around the king's tent. The number of prisoners was so large that groups of thirty were led on ropes by their captors and their value as slaves was reckoned, under the normal market conditions of supply and demand, at only three dinars each. The exchange of a prisoner for a single shoe was even recorded.

The bodies were denied burial and Reynald was executed by the sultan's own hand in revenge for his attempts on Mecca and Medina, and for his slaughter of pilgrims. Reynald had watched as Guy was offered water by Saladin, which was an indication that he would be spared. However, when he took the goblet back from the king, the sultan made it very plain that he was not offering Reynald either water or mercy.

To all intents and purposes, the Crusader field army had ceased to exist, and there was little hope for any of the cities of the kingdom. Tiberias surrendered bloodlessly the next day, followed by Acre, Nablus, Nazareth and Toron. Jaffa resisted but the entire populace was sold into slavery after it was stormed.

Tyre held out as Saladin moved onto easier prey. Sidon, Beirut and Jebail fell in early August, followed by Ascalon and Gaza. Christian refugees flocked to Tyre, and Conrad of Montferrat unexpectedly arrived with a small fleet. Conrad took command of the defence of Tyre, and a few days later Saladin paraded his father, William of Montferrat, before the city walls, threatening to kill him if Conrad did not surrender. Conrad refused but Saladin did not kill the old man.

The sultan perhaps somewhat neglected the siege of Tyre and moved to take Jerusalem. It is possible to criticise the hero of the jihad for allowing the Crusaders this foothold, but in truth he could not have predicted the ferocity of the West's response to the fall of Jerusalem. He was also unable to divert his army from the Holy City and capital of the Crusader kingdom.

Balian of Ibelin received permission from Saladin to enter Jerusalem to escort his wife and children away to the safety of Tyre, but then wrote to the sultan to say that the populace were begging him to remain in the city. Saladin's chivalry extended not only to freeing Balian from his oath, but to providing Balian's family with safe conduct to Tyre. The Muslim attack began

against the western sector of the wall, but there was fierce resistance and Saladin transferred his attack to the north. The citizens, threatened by the collapse of their walls, decided to surrender. The sultan's generous terms were quickly accepted. The city surrendered unconditionally and Latin Christians were allowed to buy their freedom at ten dinars for a man, five for a woman and one for a child. The poor were freed for a single payment of 30,000 dinars. Saladin's brother released a thousand captives that he had been awarded by the sultan and Saladin freed every elderly captive. In an act of re-sanctification, rose petals were scattered across the floor of the Dome of the Rock.

63 Naptha Grenades, a Greek invention, honed to perfection by the Muslims

Indeed, those who disbelieve in Our verses – We will drive them into a Fire. Every time their skins are roasted through We will replace them with other skins so they may taste the punishment . . .

Quran. 4:56.

The Egyptian fleet failed miserably at the siege of Tyre, and five of its ships were boarded by Frankish raiding parties from the city. The maritime fiasco demoralised Saladin's land forces, and the Muslims retreated to winter quarters at Acre. Sixty Sicilian-Norman ships entered Tyre and news came of a new and vast invasion of the Levant being planned in the West. King Guy was released, having promised to leave the Holy Land and never return. He reneged on his pledge and fled to Tyre. Tensions quickly

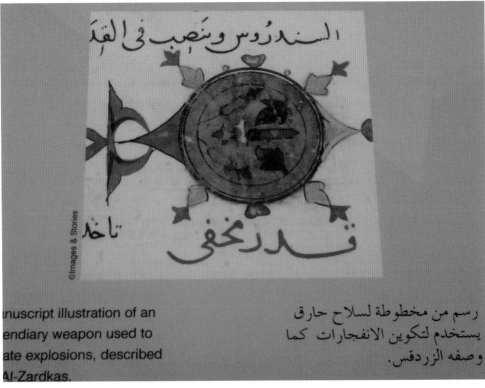

...anuscript illustration of an
...endiary weapon used to
...ate explosions, described
...Al-Zardkas.

رسم من مخطوطة لسلاح حارق
يستخدم لتكوين الانفجارات كما
وصفه الزردقس.

1 Grenades were filled with incendiary chemicals
Islamic scientists learnt the ingredients of gunpowder from the Chinese and improved its explosive effectiveness.

٠١ قذائف كانت تملأ بمواد كيميائية حارقة
نقل العلماء المسلمون خلطة البارود عن الصينيين، ثم قاموا بتطوير قدرتها التفجيرية.

2 Cannon
The earliest cannons appeared in the Muslim world during the early 8th century AH/14th century AD. Later, under the Ottomans, they became crucial in the advance of their Empire.

٠٢ مدفع
ظهر المدفع أول مرة في العالم الإسلامي في أوائل القرن الثامن الهجري/الرابع عشر الميلادي، ثم لاحقاً في العهد العثماني، صار للمدفع دور رئيس في توسع الدولة.

arose between Guy and Conrad, now the popular saviour of Tyre, and Guy marched out to besiege Acre in August 1189.

Saladin attacked the Crusader positions around Acre, and his troopers reached the city but the Crusader infantry put up a magnificent defence and pushed the Muslims out. Conrad then bought reinforcements from Tyre to Acre and a series of vicious battles ensued. In early October Templar knights came out at the charge to attack the left flank of Saladin's army. Saladin sent reinforcements from his centre. Guy saw this and made a charge. The Muslim centre caved in and the Crusaders penetrated the Muslim camp. A riderless Frank horse then caused panic in the Crusader infantry, as they thought that the knights who were plundering had been slaughtered. Saladin saw this collapse in the Crusader centre and quickly organised a charge. In the ensuing rout, the Master of the Temple was killed and Conrad had to be rescued by Guy. Three Frankish women, wearing armour and fighting in the front line, were also killed, according to the Muslim chroniclers. Then Saladin's emirs abruptly stopped their advance and surrounded him. They demanded that he send a contingent to bring back their servants, who had fled with their treasure when the Crusaders had plundered the camp. The dark comedy of errors ended as a bloody draw.

Disease spread through both camps, but the Crusaders made another attempt on the city in April 1190. Their siege towers were burnt to the ground by an anonymous man of Damascus who was an enthusiastic collector of pyrotechnic devices. His friends had often reproached and rebuked him for his passion, but he replied that it was, 'an occupation that did no harm to anyone and which

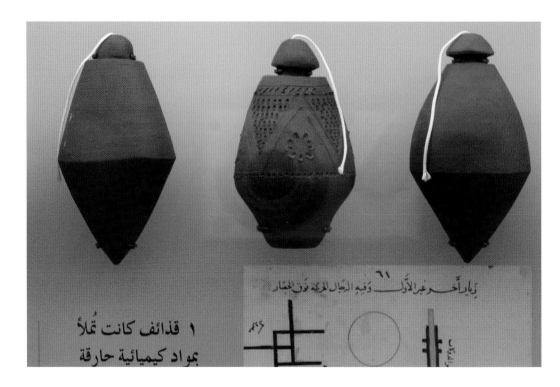

١ قذائف كانت تُملأ
بمواد كيميائية حارقة

٦١ زيار أخـــر غير الأ... وَفيه الرجال المركبة دون الغطار

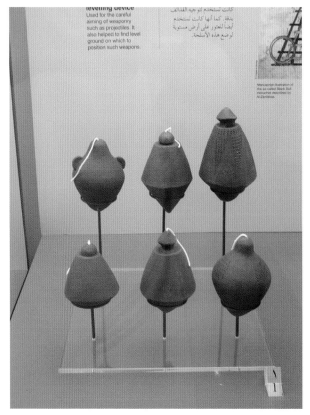

levelling device
Used for the careful
aiming of weaponry
such as projectiles. It
also helped to find level
ground on which to
position such weapons.

interested him as a hobby'. His first hits were mocked by the Crusaders, and they laughed and danced about when they saw that the containers would not make their structure burn. Unfortunately for them, he was just getting the range. His tailor-made naphtha was then loaded up and shot at the towers, exploding on impact.

The Crusaders made a mass infantry attack on 25 July but were slaughtered in their thousands. By now the siege was becoming an apocalyptic scene. The besieged garrison of Acre and the Crusaders were starving, pestilence struck at all the camps and Saladin had to retire to new positions, as the simple volume of death that had taken place between his lines and those of the Crusaders made the passage of further contagion through his troops inevitable. Despite all this, the fourth horseman, war, continued on his way.

64 The Massacre at Acre. From the Chronicle, *Overseas Passages by the French against the Turks and other Saracens*, attributed to Jean Colombe, fifteenth century

When Saladin set out to recover the ports of Syria from the Christian nations and to cleanse Jerusalem of the abomination of unbelief and to rebuild it, one fleet of unbelievers after another came to the relief of the ports. The fleet of Alexandria could not stand up against them. The Christians had had the upper hand in the eastern Mediterranean for so long, and they had numerous fleets there. The Muslims on the other hand, had for a long time been too weak to offer them any resistance.

The fourteenth-century polymath Ibn Khaldun on the Muslim loss of control of the Mediterranean in the Crusades period.

The vast Crusader army of Emperor Barbarossa broke up upon his drowning in the Anatolian River Saleph in early June 1190, and only 5,000 Germans continued on to Tyre. Henry of Champagne also brought a large contingent of French troops to the siege but their battering ram was quickly destroyed by fire, perhaps by the ingenious hobbyist of Damascus.

The winter saw Saladin running out of money and suffering from repeated fevers. His emirs were complaining about the length of the siege and all communication with the garrison was now reduced to

swimmers carrying messages, and pigeon post. The Crusader army was also desperate but Tyre, Tripoli and later Cyprus sat at the head of their supply chain, which was maintained by 500 Scandinavian ships, along with Italian squadrons.

Saladin attempted to evacuate the exhausted garrison and exchange them with fresh troops but Acre's desperate civilians rushed to the little fleet he sent, and the transports were soon too full to accommodate any but a few of the weary troops.

French and English contingents of the Third Crusade had begun to arrive in April with Philip II of France. Richard the Lionheart arrived from Cyprus, which he had taken from the Byzantines, on 12 June 1191. This was arguably his greatest contribution to the survival of Outremer. He surprisingly requested an immediate parley with Saladin. This was refused on the grounds that commanders only meet after terms are agreed, but indirect negotiations took place over three days and produced nothing. King Philip of France then led an attack on Acre, but Saladin made a diversionary attack on the eastern end of the Crusader line and the Kurdish garrison sallied valiantly out of Acre to send Phillip's men back beyond their own lines and to burn his siege engines.

Richard then brought up his siege engines, which included a gigantic mangonel named 'God's own catapult'. He began a systematic destruction of Acre's towers. The Maledicta Tower came close to collapse on 2 July 1191 and this stirred Saladin to dispatch a force of cavalry to attempt a breakthrough to the garrison on the next day, but they were held by the Crusader infantry. Saladin then instructed the garrison to attempt a breakout on the night of the 4th. However, this also failed despite a diversionary attack by the whole army. On 5 July, Richard's sappers brought the Maledicta Tower down. Unfortunately, the rubble of the tower prevented ingress into the walls and two Crusader attacks were beaten back over the next few days, but time was running out for the desperate garrison.

The garrison surrendered, and Saladin attempted to meet the obligations set by Richard – the return of the True Cross, 1,600 Crusader prisoners and a payment of 200,000 dinars – but could not. The deadline passed and rather than enslaving the prisoners, as was expected, Richard began a massacre. As many as 3,000 men were butchered. Many reasons have been given to explain the slaughter. One was that Richard killed them as a reprisal for prisoners killed by the Muslims, another was that the king had decided to march on Ascalon, and that he did not want to leave behind him these enemy soldiers. Whatever the case, another step down a very bloody path had been taken.

65 The Chertsey Abbey floor tiles of the thirteenth century. Said to depict Richard the Lionheart and Saladin in Combat

Gloucester: The trick of that voice I do well remember. Is it not the king?
Lear: Aye, every inch a king. When I do stare, see how the subject quakes.
William Shakespeare, *King Lear*, Act 4, Scene 6.

Saladin's funds were exhausted and his forces clearly feared Richard's troops. Perhaps the knowledge that the Crusaders had lost so many men at Acre buoyed the sultan at this darkest moment. He spoke

to his troops before they rode out to meet Richard's march on Ascalon: 'Only our army is facing the army of infidelity. There is none among the Muslims who will come to our succour and there is none in the lands of Islam who will help us.'

Richard was a brilliant soldier and his chosen route down the coast towards Jaffa allowed him to strike inland for Jerusalem, but also to threaten Ascalon and thereby Egypt. He was also able to transport a great deal of his supplies by ship, and the sea secured his right flank. There was no way that Saladin could counter this, as the last of his Syrian fleet had been lost to the Crusaders with the capitulation of Acre. Saladin burnt crops and destroyed the fortifications and ports at Caesarea, Arsuf and Jaffa as no men willing to defend them could be found.

Richard's column attempted to maintain an unbroken and disciplined march. The knights rode in companies, with a screen of heavy infantry covering their left flank. Saladin's troopers continually tried to break the column up, while he shadowed the Crusaders and hoped for an opportunity to launch an attack in force.

At the Nahr Zerka, the 'River of Crocodiles', Saladin mounted a major attack and tried to taunt knights out of the column to meet him on open ground, using charges against the column and archery assaults. Richard's troops kept steadfast and perfect formation, undismayed and undisturbed. Such discipline had been the key to all the Crusaders' successes in the Levant.

As Richard turned inland, Saladin's troopers took advantage of the open country and killed virtually all the Templars' horses. Richard was also wounded during a desperate defence of the column. The forests of Arsuf effected him some cover, but a battle was inevitable.

It was fought on a plateau that ended on a cliff. Richard needed to reach Arsuf by the day's end, which would put him only nine miles short of Jaffa. Saladin aimed to destroy his army. The Battle of Arsuf showed both leaders, and their men, at their very best. The Crusader infantry's discipline, opening their ranks to allow knights to charge, whilst shielding the column and taking a heavy toll of the Muslim cavalry with their crossbows, was magnificent, but Saladin's troopers also had the bit between their teeth and many even dismounted to pour more arrows into the Crusaders' ranks. Richard saw his moment and charged with his household troops. Many of the sultan's troops fled or were pushed off the cliff and into the sea. Incredibly, Saladin managed to rapidly reorganise amidst this chaos and, when the Crusader attack had begun to lose momentum, he sent his *askari* forward. They pushed the Franks back, but Richard still had an uncommitted reserve and two further Crusader charges decided the day.

The sultan re-engaged Richard only two days later, but Saladin had failed in his aim. The Crusaders reached Arsuf, and they marched from there into the ruins of Jaffa.

Daggers, Détente and Deceit

66 A Statue of Richard Couer De Lion from 1856, Houses of Parliament, London

Dear Lord, I pray Thee to suffer me not to see Thy Holy City, since I cannot deliver it from the hands of Thine enemies . . .

A prayer given up by Richard the Lionheart upon viewing the towers of Jerusalem and realising that he would never wrest the city from Saladin. Definitely apocryphal.

Saladin's brother, al-Adil, called Safadin by the Western chroniclers,* was sent to negotiate with the king against a backdrop of Phillip of France having left the Crusade and now threatening Richard's Angevin inherited lands, friction between Conrad of Montferrat and Richard over the throne of Jerusalem, and the machinations of the king's brother, John, in England. Saladin also opened talks with Conrad of Montferrat just to stir the pot a little.

The negotiations with Richard went nowhere. The king insisted on the return of the True Cross, Jerusalem and all the lands from the coast to the Jordan for peace. He did, however, offer his sister in marriage to al-Adil, with the couple to then rule Palestine.

Richard had to be stopped on the battlefield, and perhaps then a bargain could be struck. Atrocious weather aided Saladin. It slowed Richard on the road from Jaffa to Jerusalem and by early January 1192,

---

* Al-Adil's given name was Saif al-Din, or Sword of the Faith. Saladin was Salah al-Din, or the Goodness of the Faith. His full name was Salah al-Din Yusuf Ibn Ayyub, his family would have called him Yusuf.

morale in the Crusader camp was collapsing. They withdrew to the coast amid snow, hail and numerous desertions. A low-level war of attrition was fought during the spring but stalemate had ensued.

Richard tried to reinstall Guy of Lusignan on the throne of Outremer, but the barons opted instead for Conrad, and negotiations with Saladin foundered on the sultan's determination not to allow Ascalon to remain in the Franks' hands.

With a view to expediting Richard's passage home, Saladin may very well have helped Richard out with his 'Conrad problem', of which more later, but Richard still obstinately refused to quit the Levant. The draw of Jerusalem was perhaps too strong. He forced the sultan into the field at the head of a near-mutinous army with an attempt on Jerusalem on 7 June, but Saladin was able to pull troops from Damascus and Mosul and the Crusaders were pushed back to Jaffa.

Kurdish troops broke into Jaffa, but then galleys carrying Richard and his knights sailed into the harbour and Richard waded ashore despite a fierce archery fusillade. He rapidly drove the Muslims from Jaffa. Saladin attempted a night attack to kill the king, but it failed amid infighting between Kurds and Turks and the Muslims then faced a 'hedgehog' of Crusader infantry spearmen backed by crossbowmen, with Richard's cavalry drawn up behind.

Surprisingly, given the morale of the army and the fact that their dead were piling up, the Turks and Kurds kept coming on. Richard launched a cavalry charge, but the Muslims refused to yield the field and came close to victory in the ensuing battle. The Crusader resistance continued until dusk, and, strictly speaking, Richard won the day, but he had gained very little for his efforts. The king fell sick and rushed into a treaty. By the terms of the accord the Crusaders were given pilgrim access to Jerusalem, and possession of the coast from Acre to Jaffa, but Ascalon returned to Saladin's possession. Richard hurried back to Europe without ever entering Jerusalem.

67 Soap from Aleppo, a luxury enjoyed by Crusaders, and their ladies

He gives to each of them a poniard of terrible length and sharpness. From their devoted obedience, they never hesitate to set out as they are commanded; nor do they pause until they have reached the prince, or tyrant, who has been pointed out to them; and they remain in his service until they find a favourable opportunity for accomplishing their purpose, believing that by so doing they shall gain the favour of heaven . . .

A troubadour's description of how the Assassin Grand Master would prepare his *fidai* for their deadly work. From the *Carmen Ambrosii*.

Conrad was very much the first man in Palestine. He had married Isabella, the daughter of Amalric, probably against her will, and this essentially made him co-regent of Jerusalem with baronial support, though Guy of Lusignan refused to abdicate. He had the support of Philip of France, but Richard the Lionheart backed Guy, and after Philip's departure Richard attempted the role of kingmaker.

He failed during an assembly in April 1192, as the barons who attended the meeting unanimously voted for Conrad. Richard seemed to accept the decision, and compensated Guy with Cyprus, but he certainly kept his hopes for a friend on the throne of Jerusalem alive through the person of his nephew, Henry of Champagne.

As we have seen, al-Adil and Richard had negotiated frequently, and Saladin had extensive contacts with the Assassin Grand Master, Sinan. Furthermore, Conrad had made proposals to Saladin for a coalition against Richard, and 700 of Richard's knights had deserted him for service under Conrad during the retreat from Jerusalem to Jaffa. Richard still threatened both Jerusalem and Egypt. His departure from the Holy Land could perhaps be speeded along if Conrad could be removed.

Isabella has obtained a reputation for enjoying her baths too much and for lingering in the tub. In fairness to the lady bathing was a virtual art in the Middle East completed by fine Aleppan soaps made of natural olive oil boiled in vats with water, lye and laurel oil and allowed to cool and dry for up to nine months. On the night of his killing Conrad had tired of waiting for his wife's ablutions to end and had gone out alone. Of course, it is de rigueur for the medieval monks who were the recorders of such events to blame a woman, but the fact remains that whilst Conrad was murdered by Sinan's men, Isabella was one of any number of likely accessories to the fact.

Saladin probably commissioned Sinan to have Conrad killed. Given the near exhaustion of Saladin's resistance to Richard, he needed it done quickly. The marquis had also offended Sinan by seizing a cargo ship belonging to the Assassins and had added further insult by drowning its crew.

Suspicion also falls on Henry of Champagne. He had a long relationship with Sinan and had even witnessed two *fidai'in* showing their dedication to their master by leaping from one of Masyaf's battlements to their deaths. Henry married Conrad's widow within a week of the killing and was acclaimed King of Jerusalem in May 1192. The Templars and Hospitallers also had a vested interest in Conrad's demise. They favoured Guy re-ascending the throne. He had proved himself a weak king, whilst Conrad came from a powerful Crusading 'dynasty'. Conrad's brother was a Palestinian Baron and his nephew, Boniface, would be a leading participant in the Fourth Crusade. Beyond that the Genoese favoured Conrad, whilst their deadly rivals, the Pisans, favoured Guy.

French writers state how, when tortured, a surviving Assassin claimed that he had acted on behalf of Richard. English versions of the murder have Conrad dying in the arms of his faithful wife, who presumably had by now finished her bath.

68 The Two Tombs of Saladin in the Great Mosque of Damascus. The original twelfth-century wooden sarcophagus, and an early twentieth-century marble gift of dubious aesthetic value donated by Kaiser Wilhelm II

This duty has been placed upon me, it is my job, and with God's help I shall take the most determined and resolute course . . .

Saladin on the jihad and the contest with the Crusaders.

In March 1193, Saladin died in Damascus. He was not a great battlefield general. He failed at Mont Gisard, Ramla and Jaffa, and he lost Acre, but he was a great war leader. His political acumen and intelligence-gathering was the key to his victory at Hattin, and his personal attributes and selfless commitment to the jihad was what maintained his army in the field throughout the long, unrewarding contest against the Third Crusade. The last years of his life were spent on the battlefield in an exhausting

defence of Islam and yet he still upheld the highest standards of civil governance. Following Nur al-Din's example, he maintained the rule of law and gave an example of moral leadership that was the antithesis of almost every other government of the time. At times his actions were those of a man tilting at windmills, but his naive attachment to an ideal meant that he achieved epic feats which mere generalship could not have accomplished.

When discussing the terms of the final treaty with Richard, Saladin had said to his emirs:

We have become accustomed to fighting the Holy War and indeed we have achieved our aim. Now it is difficult to break off what has become customary . . . we have no other occupation other than that of making war . . . If we

give up this work what shall we do? If we destroy our hope of defeating them, what shall we hope for? I am afraid that with nothing to do death will overcome me . . . my feeling is to reject the idea of a truce and in preferring war to prefer my honour and make it my leader . . .

His emirs had replied:

Divine grace assists you but you alone have looked to yourself as one accustomed to happiness, to the desire to serve God, to the acquisition of eternal virtue. In yourself you find a force and tenacity, and your indestructible faith marks you out as one to achieve the aims we strive for. But look too at the state of the country, ruined and trampled underfoot and your subjects beaten down, at your armies exhausted and sick, at your horses neglected and ruined. Food is in short supply, and the necessities of life are dear, the rich are reduced to hunger, the poor to destitution. Straw is more precious than gold, barley unobtainable at any price.

And if the Franj *fail to get the truce they will devote all their energies to strengthening and consolidating their position. They will face death with high courage in the course of achieving their aims, and for love of their faith they will refuse to submit to humiliation. The best thing is for you to remember the verse revealed by God, 'and if they incline to peace you too should incline to it.'*

Saladin therefore left war to one side for the good of his people and of his soldiers and went to Jerusalem and then on to retire in Damascus. In simple terms, and without even throwing into the equation his near-bloodless conquest of the Holy City, Saladin's personal talents and character confirm him as the greatest hero of the Crusades.

69 An Ayyubid-period incense burner with Christian iconography, a rare example of cultural exchange between the Crusader kingdoms and their Muslim adversaries

The unjustly treated merchants, kiss the earth in the exalted presence of the Lord, the ruler, the Sultan al-Adil, may God prolong his days, unfurl in distant lands of the earth his banners, appoint the heavenly angels to assist his armies, and the kings of the earth to serve as his slaves; They intended to leave [Alexandria], but were prevented from this with the pretext that they were from Cyprus. None of them is from Cyprus, they being Pisans and Venetians and one from Beirut . . . they had traded the greater part of their merchandise for buri fish, which has perished so that they had to throw it away. They ask for mercy from the sultan . . .

A petition from Italian merchants to al-Adil describing their complex position. There was war between Egypt and Cyprus, but not between Egypt and Crusader Palestine.

Saladin had seventeen sons and a host of other male relatives. The history of the period following his death is confused and complex, and dominated by internecine warfare between his Ayyubid successors. During this time the unity achieved by Saladin between the major centres of Islamic power, Damascus, Aleppo, Egypt and the Jazira, dissolved. Egypt's hegemony slowly increased, since it was the only entity that Saladin had had enough time to reconstruct as a sophisticated state, with well-functioning ministries and bureaus. There was also a growing reliance on Mamluks in the armies of the Ayyubids, along with an increasingly large political role for the army in their states.

Of Saladin's sons, al-Afdal took Damascus, al-Zahir gained Aleppo and al-Aziz acquired Egypt. Al-Adil took the northern territories but used his history with the *Salahiyya* – the old *askari* of Saladin – to take Damascus and then usurp Egypt upon the death of al-Aziz. The Crusaders did not interfere, Outremer had been militarily drained by the Third Crusade and détente benefited everyone.

There was some fighting over coastal possessions with the arrival of German Crusaders at the close of the century but a truce of five years was concluded, and as we will see below, though Pope Innocent III called for Crusade against Egypt in 1202, this venture ended up striking Constantinople and not Cairo.

Al-Adil was able to keep the peace despite having to negotiate with two more kings of Jerusalem and among the murky politics of Crusader regencies and thrones held in queens' names, but could do nothing to prevent the Fifth Crusade landing on Egypt's shores in May 1218. The Crusaders attacked Damietta over the next 14 months, and al-Kamil took over the defence from his father when al-Adil died. So frantic was al-Kamil that he offered the Crusaders the restoration of all lands west of the Jordan, and upon the fall of Damietta he threw Jerusalem into the pot.

In early spring the Crusaders refused even al-Kamil's added desperate offer of the return of the True Cross. This was a mistake as a recent rebellion of emirs in the Jazira had finally been put down, which released the forces of Damascus and Mosul for service in Egypt, and the flood season was beginning. In July the Crusaders attempted an advance up the Nile. The army had 5,000 knights and 40,000 infantry, supported by over 600 ships. There was panic in Cairo but al-Kamil turned the Crusaders back and via a tributary of the Nile he managed to get the army of Damascus between the Frankish army and Damietta. By mid-August the Franks were surrounded and running out of supplies. Al-Kamil then launched an attack down the Nile with galleys sailing down the river alongside the army, and opened the Nile floodgates. Lightly-armed Nubian auxiliaries hunted stragglers through the boggy floodplains, as the Crusaders attempted to retreat from the apocalyptic landscape.

The Crusaders still held Damietta, and al-Kamil offered the return of the True Cross and safe passage from Egypt in exchange for its return. The Crusaders had gambled and lost the Holy City, but they would obtain it again through the strangest of circumstances.

The Capella Palatina, Palermo, Sicily, twelfth century

Why did the muezzins not give the call to prayer in the normal way last night? ... My chief aim in passing the night in Jerusalem was to hear the call to prayer given by the muezzins, and their cries of praise to God during the night ...

The Holy Roman Emperor Frederick II Barbarossa complaining
to the chief *qadi* of Jerusalem at his decision to stop the muezzins
calling prayer for fearing of ruining the Emperor's sleep.

The Capella Palatina was not Frederick's creation, but he was the perfect man to inherit it, created as it was from a blending of three traditions with a *muqarnas* or wooden stalactite Fatimid-style ceiling, Byzantine mosaics in the upper parts of its walls, and magnificent Norman doors.

Frederick, like the chapel, was a curious amalgam of the three cultures, and though the popular claim that he spoke six languages is a little dubious, he was certainly one of the most cosmopolitan rulers of the Middle Ages. He had a vision of the world that excelled almost any other politician in Europe at the time, and his Crusade of 1228 to the Holy Land turned out to be very different in nature to any other. His character was as complex as the little political world of Outremer that he entered after

he obtained the throne of Jerusalem in 1225 through marriage to Isabella II, the daughter of John of Brienne, who had himself taken the throne only after marriage to Maria, the posthumous daughter of King Henry.

Such was al-Kamil's concern over Frederick coming to power in Acre, and the fact that the emperor also had the impressive fleet of Sicily to back any threat he made against Muslim possessions, that in 1226 he sent an embassy offering the return of all the territories taken by Saladin. By this act al-Kamil hoped to prevent the launching of another Crusade against Egypt, and he was in fact not giving away anything *he* owned, these lands were his brother al-Muazzam's, with whom he was at loggerheads.

Then Fredrick, amongst much wrangling with the pope over funds and lands, was excommunicated. In fact in 1227 Frederick had been building up forces in Brindisi to take on the Holy War and had even funded the venture with 100,000 ounces of gold, and employed 1,000 knights, though it seems to have taken some arm-twisting by Pope Honorius III to make the emperor bear the costs of the venture. However, a plague decimated his force before it could depart.

Frederick's excommunication by the pope and papal threats against Sicily made the danger of an armed Crusade unlikely. Yet, when Frederick arrived in the Levant in 1229 without an army, he was still courted by al-Kamil. Al-Kamil was now in control of Jerusalem and, in the treaty of Jaffa, he gave it to Frederick, along with Bethlehem. He retained the Dome of the Rock and the al-Aqsa mosque as a Muslim enclave. The two men seem to have got along extremely well; they were much of a kind, Machiavellian before the word had even been coined, and far-sighted politically.

Contemporary Muslims were appalled by the treaty and Christians were equally disgusted, but al-Kamil knew that Jerusalem was the draw for the Crusades that had, and could continue to, assail his lands. Dispensing with it allowed him to look to other distant, but far larger concerns. The armies of the Mongol Khans were already marching west, and if they came to the Levant, peace with the Franks might just be the first step to an alliance against this far more deadly foe.

New Jerusalems and New Enemies

71 The Four Horses of the Constantinople Hippodrome in their current home of the museum of the cathedral of San Marco, Venice, c. third century

To its initiators it seemed that one part of the army should be sent to the eastern regions, another to Spain and a third against the Slavs . . .

Helmond of Bosau, writing as a contemporary of the Second Crusade on the idea of a universal Crusade.

The Crusades were launched to bring succour to Eastern Christians, but the relationship between Byzantines and Latins had been acrimonious from Bohemond and Alexius' intrigues and confrontations through to the massacre of the Latins in Constantinople in 1182. The Normans, major players in the Crusades, continually assaulted the Empire, with Roger of Sicily invading Greece in 1147. Venice overtook Byzantium as the dominant naval power in the Mediterranean before the Crusades, and by 1082 the emperor was compelled to create a toll-free harbour for the Venetians. In 1125 and 1175 the Byzantines hesitated to renew the lease and the Republic ravaged their coastline and islands until the emperor conceded. Outremer also took away trade, and revenue, from Constantinople.

There was also in Western Europe a new confidence and perhaps even

a conscious feeling of 'destiny' that had been growing since the beginning of the eleventh century. The threats of the Vikings, the Muslims of North Africa and the Hungarians were fading, and Outremer gave an entry point into the Near East trade system. The rise of centralised monarchies, of internal trade, and the taming of the worst excesses of the feudal system were matched by a technological evolution in agriculture that brought large tracts of land under the plough. The Fourth Crusade was therefore a microcosm of the wider action of the Crusades period: a period that saw the usurpation of Greek power in the Eastern Mediterranean by Western European powers, Polish-German expansion into Eastern Europe with settlements in Prussia, and the pushing back of Muslim Spain.

Then there were the claims of Holy Roman Emperors like Henry VI to universal rule over Christendom, and of popes who now held four of the five patriarchates: Alexandria, Antioch, Jerusalem and Rome. Only Constantinople remained outside of their grasp.

The papal indulgence was also changing its nature. Indeed, the format of the indulgence for the Fourth Crusade differed markedly from that of previous *expeditiones*. The notion of pleasing God through meritorious martial works rather than simply liberating the Holy Sepulchre was introduced, and this allowed for an even greater degree of flexibility in the use of the Crusade weapon. This was soon applied to internal enemies of the Church in the Albigensian Crusade of 1208.

The Crusader Villehardouin tells us that many men took the cross for the Fourth Crusade because the indulgence was so great, but this would have been devalued by the hugely increased cost of Crusading in the early thirteenth century. It did not take much for the Venetian Doge, Dandolo, to convince the knights of the Crusade that supplementing their funds by a raid on Constantinople on the way to the Holy Land would benefit everyone.

The notion of being 'God's people' diminished the importance of pilgrimage to the Holy Places, and replaced it with the 'holy right' of Latins as holders of the one true Catholic faith to conquer unbelievers. Robert of Clari later justified the sack of Constantinople by the need to remove the relics from the schismatic Greeks to the safety of the West. Byzantium was about to fall victim to this universal Crusade.

 ## The Basilica of Christ's Blood, Bruges, twelfth century

When twice six hundred years and fifty more
Are gone since the blessed Mary's son was born,
Then Antichrist shall come full of the devil.

> The thirteenth-century chronicler Matthew of Paris predicting the Sixth Age.

A fever for relics overtook Europe in the thirteenth century. It may have been due to a consistent feeling running though society from top to bottom that the Sixth Age was coming which ended

Christological history as interpreted from the Bible. Alternatively, as I have suggested above, it was an awakening idea that Jerusalem and the Holy Land was in fact a spiritual realm that was more locally European and solidly Catholic than the ephemeral Holy City far away over the seas.

The springing-up of cities such as San Sepolcro in Tuscany, where relics taken from Jerusalem in the late eleventh and early twelfth century formed the nucleus of new towns, was not that

uncommon but there was an acceleration in the thirteenth century with entire buildings being built to house one relic, as with this delightful chapel in Bruges built to house a phial of Christ's blood.

The Fourth Crusade was a reflection of all this, but it also created a Latin Empire in Greece that was doomed to fail from the outset. Throughout its brief life it was chronically short of manpower and money and appears to have been unattractive even to adventurers from the West. Pope Gregory IX even resorted to pleading with the Count of Brittany to Crusade for the Latin Emperor rather than for Outremer. Henry of Romania neatly summarised the situation, 'there is nothing lacking to complete possession of the Empire save an abundance of Latins'.

Any actions of the Latin Emperor were also hampered by a constitution that favoured the Venetians and fief holders far more than the central authority. The Latin Empire failed to gain the support of the emerging Balkan states such as the Bulgars because of what we might today term confessionalism but what was to the medieval mind a much more straightforward question of faith, salvation and identity. Identity was a potent concept in the Middle Ages and particularly so in the Balkans. The sometimes vicious attempts to suppress religious dissent in this period make sense as long as we keep this idea of identity in mind. Mediaeval communities were defined by their religion, and religion also demarcated each community's political allegiances. Leaders who deviated from their faith risked losing all allegiance from their lords and from the populace. As we will see a little later, it was not for nothing that Thomas Aquinas compared those who slipped from the true faith to counterfeiters, as both eroded the secular foundations of society.

One slightly odd consequence of the Latin Empire of Constantinople was that it actually strengthened the Byzantines in Anatolia as many of the aristocratic families fleeing the capital relocated to Trebizond and took their monies and feudal levies with them. This pushed back the advances of the Saljuq Turks who had been pressuring the border since the Battle of Myriokephalon. This proved to be an effective buffer for the city of Constantinople when Anatolia collapsed into chaos with the coming of the Mongols in 1241, perhaps the relic collectors of Western Europe were correct, holy objects did need to be saved before the coming of the Antichrist.

A Mamluk Bombard or Grenade, carrying remarkable engraving and artistry for what is essentially a bomb, thirteenth century

We were all covered with fire-darts. By good luck, I found a thick Saracen's tunic. I made a shield of the tunic, which served me in good stead, for their fire-darts only wounded me in five places and my pony in fifteen ... There was a patch of ground behind the Templars, the size of a day's work, so covered with the darts that the Saracens had thrown, that the soil could not be seen for the density of them ...

The Lord Jean de Joinville describing the firestorm of ordnance hurled at the Crusaders at al-Mansura by the *Bahriyya* Mamluk regiment.

Calls for a new Crusade following the despoiling of the Holy Sepulchre and the disastrous Battle of Harbiyya (of which more later) brought Louis IX of France and an army of 20,000 men to Egypt's shores in 1249. Louis put a large force ashore near Damietta on 5 June, and the city fell the following day.

Louis waited out the flood season and marched on Cairo on 20 November. Despite being gravely ill, al-Salih prepared defences at al-Mansura with his *Bahriyya* Mamluks. Al-Salih died on 24 November. His heir, Turanshah, was far away in the Jazira. The sultan's widow concealed his death and forged a decree naming the senior emir, Al-Shuyukh, commander-in-chief. Al-Shuyukh was an elderly but inspiring leader and he halted the Crusader advance at al-Mansura. He then moved his siege engines to the riverbank. The Crusaders endeavoured to bridge the river and the Mamluks stopped them dead with a barrage of grenades and short *naft* darts fired from tubes mounted on their bows – three darts could be loaded into the tube and fired simultaneously.

On 7 February 1249, the Crusaders discovered a ford upstream and the king's brother charged along the river after crossing, took the Muslim encampment on the river by surprise and stormed into the city itself. The Mamluks were initially scattered, but then very rapidly barricaded the streets to prevent the Crusaders' withdrawal and killed virtually the entire force in hand-to-hand fighting.

The *Bahriyya*, under the junior emir Baybars, moved out of al-Mansura to meet the rest of the king's forces. The fighting lasted for the rest of the day. The Mamluks poured arrows and *naft* darts into the Crusaders' ranks, and Louis charged again and again to relieve the pressure on his infantry. A late deployment of his crossbowmen won the day for Louis, as he managed to hold the riverbank, but the campaign was slipping away from him. Muslim reinforcements were arriving by the hour at al-Mansura. The Franks constructed a pontoon bridge to unite their now-outnumbered forces.

The *Bahriyya* launched an assault on 11 February and overwhelmed many of the Crusaders' positions, but they failed to burn the pontoon bridge, despite the use of glass grenades filled with *naft*. Al-Shuyukh died and the new sultan, Turanshah, did not arrive at al-Mansura until 28 February, so command devolved to a clique of Mamluk emirs. A flotilla of small boats was then transported on the backs of camels downstream of the Crusaders. This little fleet very effectively cut the Crusader supply line from Damietta. Soon enough, the river and the Crusader lines were full of corpses: starvation and the filth surrounding them combined to cause contagion in the Frankish camp.

Louis offered to exchange Damietta for Jerusalem; this was rejected out of hand and he started a retreat on 5 April 1250. The Mamluks chased his army down the river and killed several thousand of his men. The rest of the Crusaders, including a gravely ill Louis, surrendered. The Mamluks massacred all the sick troops. A Mamluk Sultanate was then called into being by Baybars's murder of the sultan Turanshah. The next half-century would be one of the bloodiest periods of Middle-Eastern history.

Modern-Day Celebrations of Ponies and Bactrian Camels, the animals that helped to create the Mongol Empire

The crown of the caliphate and the house whereby the rites of the Faith were exalted is laid waste by desolation.

There appear in the morning light traces of the assault of decay in its habitation, and tears have left their marks upon its ruins.

O, fire of my heart, for a fire of clamorous war that blazed out upon it, when a whirlwind smote the habitation!

High stands the Cross over the tops of its minbars, and he whom a girdle used to confine has become master . . .

> Ibn Abul-Yusr, a contemporary poet of Damascus, writing of the massacre and destruction of Baghdad by Hulegu Khan in 1258, and Muslim fears that the Mongols would bring with them Christian rule.

Prester John's armies were finally coming, and thanks to their ponies and camels and the sheep that provided meat-on-the-hoof, they were coming quickly and en masse. In 1206 Chinggis Khan was proclaimed universal khan of the Mongolian tribes, and in the 1220s they thrust through Russia and into eastern Persia. By 1227 a Mongol offensive reached western Islam. In 1238 caliphal embassies were sent from Baghdad to France and England to seek alliances against the invaders, but these were rebuffed as there was confidence in Europe that the Mongols either were, or would become, Christians. Those 'in the field' attempting these conversions knew better. The Franciscan William of Rubruck wrote:

> *The monk told me that the Khan believes only the Christians, but that he wants everybody to pray for him. The monk lied, for the Khan believes in no one, as you shall soon learn . . .*

A ramshackle but large state, the Khwarazmian Shahnate, had emerged from the ruins of the eastern Saljuq Empire but by 1237 it was in its death throes as the Mongols smashed through it on their way to Anatolia, where at the Battle of Kose Dagh they extinguished the western Saljuq states. Khwarazmian troopers rapidly became soldiers of fortune and headed west, seeking employment with the petty Ayyubid rulers, who were building armies to resist the Mongols and to attack each other.

Khwarazmian freebooters stopped off at Jerusalem on their way to join Sultan al-Salih in Cairo. They breached the city's walls, massacred monks and nuns and killed the city governor. The citadel's garrison appealed to Acre, but after receiving no reply they sent to al-Nasir, the Emir of Nablus, who negotiated safe passage from the city for the populace in exchange for the citadel's surrender. Two thousand Christians later returned to the city after seeing Crusader pennants flying from the citadel, but it was a Khwarazmian ruse and they were massacred under the city walls. The Khwarazmians then desecrated the tombs of the Latin kings and set fire to the Church of the Holy Sepulchre.

The devastation of Jerusalem's holy places brought Crusaders from every part of the kingdom to form the last great army that Outremer would ever put into the field. Muslim Syria allied with the Crusaders in the hope of ridding themselves of al-Salih, and battle was joined at Harbiyya in northern Gaza on 17 October 1244.

The allied army attacked immediately upon sighting the Egyptians. They had the advantage of numbers. The Franks formed the right flank of the army, Damascus, Homs and Nablus made up the

centre and left wing. The *Bahriyya* Mamluks broke the Franks' charge and then the Khwarazmians, who had been mustered out to the extreme right of the Mamluks, swung down upon the Ayyubids and the allies' entire left disintegrated. The troops of Damascus panicked and fled, the Crusaders then turned in disgust on their Ayyubid allies, and a battle within the battle ensued. A Khwarazmian charge then pushed the Crusaders and the men of Homs into the Mamluks, who massacred them with mace and axe. The Crusaders lost 6,000 men, a loss which would soon be grievously felt.

75 The Eleventh-Century Friday Mosque in Qazvin. Men, women and children were slaughtered in concentration camps that the Mongols set up outside Qazvin during their destruction of the Assassins Order. Even babes in their cradles were murdered

Neither people, nor corn, nor food, nor clothing . . . the people ate only human flesh, dogs and cats for a whole year because the warriors of Chinggis Khan had burnt down the granaries . . .

The fourteenth-century Iranian writer Saifi.

The blood spilt at Harbiyya and al-Mansura was as nothing to what was to take place in Baghdad, where the Tigris would be choked with bodies. In 1256 the Great Mongol Khan, Mongke, had tasked his brother, Hulegu, with exterminating the Ismaili Assassins of Persia in revenge for an attempt on the Great Khan's life, and with bringing the Caliph of Baghdad to submission. The first part of Hulegu's mission was fairly well completed by the beginning of 1258.

In February 1258 Hulegu moved against Baghdad. He deceived the caliph's army with a probe and a feigned retreat to lure it into marshy land. The caliphal army was encircled and massacred almost to a man. It seems that the Caliph al-Mustasim was not the brightest Abbasid to have sat on the throne of Baghdad, and he harboured the illusion that the Mongols would do no harm to the leader of the

faithful, saying, 'Baghdad is enough for me, and they will not begrudge it me if I renounce all the other countries to them. Nor will they attack me when I am in it, for it is my house and my residence.' Upon his capture he was rolled up in a carpet and kicked to death. The Mongols never spilt royal blood directly.

Hulegu moved on to accept the peaceful submission of Armenia and Georgia. Mosul made obeisance and the Saljuqs of Anatolia put their forces at Hulegu's disposal. Aleppo was taken, and its fate was as bloody as Baghdad's. Damascus capitulated upon the Mongols' approach and Islam was disestablished as the official religion of the area. Bohemond VI of Antioch submitted to Hulegu and was swiftly excommunicated by Acre's papal legate. Hulegu then sent envoys to Cairo, demanding surrender.

The Mamluks who held Cairo following Baybars's murder of Turanshah had initially elected al-Salih's widow to rule as queen of the Muslims, but the coup leaders could not gain the full support of the army, and there was even a faction within the *Bahriyya* that attempted to kill Baybars for his regicide.

The junta selected a senior emir, Aybeg, as commander-in-chief, and arrested all the Kurdish emirs, for fear that they might remain pro-Ayyubid. Shajar al-Durr was forced to abdicate in favour of Aybeg, who was then replaced only five days later by al-Ashraf Musa, a 10-year-old great nephew of al-Salih, supported by a clique of emirs. Aybeg then made a political marriage with Shajar al-Durr, as the state split into factions. Aybeg garnered enough support to become *atabeg* to the child sultan and calls for unity in 1253 upon news of the Mongol army being built for Islam's destruction stabilised his

rule. His right-hand man, Qutuz, then killed the leader of Baybars's faction. Baybars and 700 troopers fled to Syria to become swords for hire. Aybeg meanwhile sought a better political marriage but Shajar al-Durr had him slain in his bath in April 1257. She herself was killed within the same month and her body was found outside Cairo's citadel, the victim of a faction led by Qutuz that had put her stepson up as heir. Egypt did not look ready to take on the Mongol superpower.

Islam Saves Europe, but at a Price

 76 **A Lustreware Plaque from an Iranian Ilkhanid *mihrab* c. 1300–1350. Vicious Mongol persecution of Islam had, by the turn of the century, been replaced by conversion**

The Mongols conquered the land and there came to them
From Egypt a Turk, who sacrificed his life.
In Syria he destroyed and scattered them.
To everything there is a pest of its own kind.

Abu Shama writing c. 1260.

The Mongols threatened the extinguishing of Islam in its traditional lands, and if Egypt fell and gave access to the Mediterranean the conquest of southern Europe was the logical sequelae. The action of Sultan Qutuz, killing Hulegu's envoys carrying Hulegu's letter:

Say to Egypt, Hulegu has come, with swords unsheathed and sharp.
The mightiest of her children will become humble, He will send their children to join the aged . . .

by cutting them in half in the horse market, might seem reckless but the sultan really had no other option but resistance. Submission would mean exile to the bloodthirsty desert. Another factor in favour of making a stand was the reappearance of Baybars and his exiled *Bahriyya* in March 1260 under an oath of safety. Every man counted now; there were only 24,000 cavalrymen in Egypt and perhaps 30,000 more in Syria. More important than the return of Qutuz's favourite enemy, however, was that Hulegu had retired from Syria with a very large part of his forces in August 1259 to watch more closely events further east. Mongke, the Great Khan, had died and Hulegu's brothers Qubilai and Ariq Boke were prepared to undertake war on each other for the succession.

Ariq Boke was backed by the Genghisid family in Mongolia and by the Golden Horde's khan, Berke, whilst Qubilai held the support of most of the generals of the Mongol army and China, the Mongols' most prized possession. What really concerned Hulegu was that Berke's forces lay directly to his north in the Caucasus. There was already antipathy between the two junior khans over rights of conquest in Persia but Berke had also converted to Islam whilst Hulegu had continued with persecutions. Hulegu therefore went to Maragha to meet any incursion by the Golden Horde. For the Mamluks he was far enough away to give them at least a chance against the remainder of his force that he had left behind under Kit Buqa, one of his most experienced and trusted lieutenants, to mop up Syria.

Kit Buqa's move down towards Egypt effectively led to the surrounding of the Crusader state, and it became obvious to the Crusaders that the Mongols' arrival in Syria would not herald any immediate change in their fortunes.

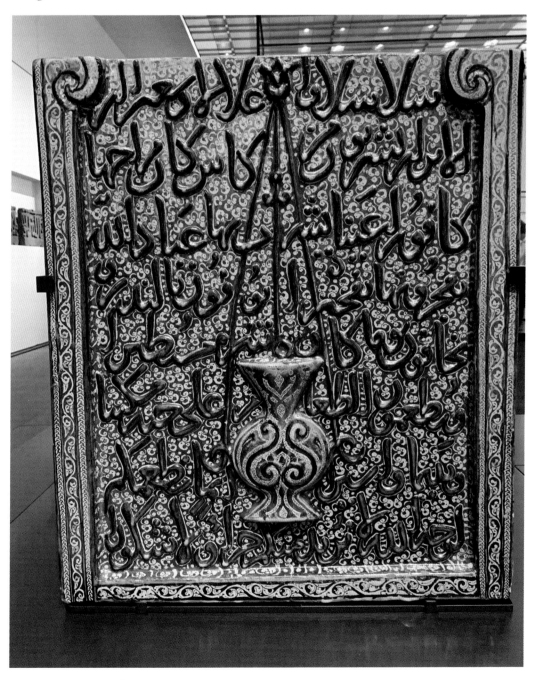

Qutuz had his Mamluks, contingents of left-over Khwarazmians, Ayyubid soldiers, Kurds, Bedouins and Turcomen refugees from the Mongols, and decided to seize the moment but he and Baybars had to shame and to beat many of the men to get them to march.

Emirs of the Muslims! For a long time you have been eating the money of the treasury and now you don't want to fight. I, myself will set out. He who chooses the Holy War will accompany me; he who does not can go home. God observes him, and the guilt of those who violate the women of the Muslims will be on the heads of the laggards!

It was only when Qutuz made his preparations to leave and said, 'I am going to fight the Mongols alone', that they followed him out of Cairo's citadel on the march to Syria.

77   Mamluk Helmets, or possibly Ottoman copies made to revere the Dynasty that Defeated the Mongols

As man is built of four foundations: namely bone, flesh, blood and arteries, so is the compound bow in as much as wood to bone, horn to flesh, sinews to arteries and glue to blood . . .
From an archery manual of the Mamluk Sultanate.

Baybars and Qutuz decided the Mamluk strategy. They would come far enough north along the Palestinian coast so that they would be able to then move inland sharply to cut the Mongol lines of communication if Kit Buqa should decide to try to strike south towards Egypt. Qutuz sent an embassy to the Franks of Acre to ensure safe passage for his forces through Crusader lands. Only the Master of the Teutonic Order warned against it, and perhaps it is surprising that the Crusaders chose the Mamluks over the Mongols, but if the Mamluks were unwelcome guests, were the Mongols any better? Despite Crusader appeasement Kit Buqa had raided Sidon and destroyed fortified centres in Syria and the Transjordan. Syria was clearly, to the Mongols, just another colony to be pacified without reference to *any* of its inhabitants. The *Gestes de Chiprois* also tells us that the

Franks were offered the horses of the Mongols should the Mamluks defeat them. Perhaps this swung them in favour of the Egyptians; after all, business is business.

Kit Buqa crossed the Jordan and entered Galilee, encamping at Ayn Jalut, the Spring of Goliath, at the foot of Mount Gilboa. The Mamluks marched through Nazareth and arrived at Ayn Jalut shortly after the Mongols. The battle proper began on 3 September. The Mongols took up position on the plain near the spring and the Mamluks rode forward to meet them. The Mongol line ran north to south across the valley and was anchored on its left by Mount Gilboa; their Ayyubid 'allies' were positioned on its extreme left wing ready to form the second assault rather than the first. The Mongol right very quickly defeated the Mamluk

left under Baybars, perhaps too quickly, as the Mongols then found themselves under heavy assault by the troopers of Qutuz's bodyguard, sending the Mongol right into disorder. The Qipchaq Turks knew just as well as the Mongols how to use provocation to draw the enemy on. Kit Buqa, however, was far from beaten and he reorganised his forces so quickly that he was nearly able, within only a short time, to turn the battle. Qutuz threw off his helmet so that his troops could see him clearly and led a frontal charge as he called out the battle cry, 'Oh Islam! Allah! Help your servant Qutuz!' This threw the Mongols into disarray, and then the Ayyubids deserted them.

The bloody battle lasted from dawn till midday and changed from combat to annihilation. A detachment of Mongols fled the battle but were pursued by Baybars and slaughtered at the top of a hill just clear of the main battlefield. The Mamluks set fire to reed beds near the small river that runs through the valley to flush out Mongols who were either hiding in them or trying to escape across the river. Local villagers killed many of them as they fled. The debacle was completed by either the death or capture of Kit Buqa. It seems most likely that he was killed during Qutuz's final charge but the chroniclers have him being beheaded by Qutuz after prophesising Qutuz's murder by his own comrades.

78 Banners of Mamluk Sultans, used to rally and to direct the best soldiers of the Middle Ages

An arrow from a warrior
Shot at an unbeliever
Counts more than the endless prayers
Said by a pious hermit.

A passage from a Mamluk war manual capturing how successful
jihad justified military government.

What was left of the Mongol army fled north to find sanctuary with the King of Armenia. Damascus, Hama and Aleppo were abandoned. Baybars chased the Mongols through the north of the country, and defeated a contingent of 2,000 troops that Hulegu had belatedly sent to Kit Buqa's aid.

At Ayn Jalut there were two charges by the Mamluks under Qutuz but these were not planned and launched from a defensive position as at al-Mansura, but made in the heat of a fluid, fast-moving cavalry battle. Qutuz's first charge was against a Mongol contingent that was flushed

with its success in defeating the Mamluk left wing and was therefore vulnerable to a charge; his second charge was against Kit Buqa's hastily-formed counter-attack. Both were timed to perfection. Mamluk battlefield communications were impressive for the period and they were guided by their banners and drums. At Ayn Jalut the Mamluks had no close-support infantry to cover them while they organised as European knights would, and certainly there was very little time for them to form up methodically. Their charges were organised literally on the hoof, and yet they were delivered to maximum effect. The battle was won by what had been instilled on the training ground, and the training ground and the hippodrome, or *maydan*, was where a Mamluk spent most of his life.

Captured as boys, shipped to Cairo by the Genoese commonly, and bought by an *ustadh* or master, and then manumitted, every Mamluk novice trained the same way. They learned how to make the 'Falcon's Talons' to grip the bow and practised without arrows for several days. Novices then moved on to a featherless arrow that was shot over and over again at almost point-blank range at a cotton-filled leather tube called the *buttiya*. They would progress through five bows of increasing draw-weight. The final one was the *qaws* used for combat. Novices memorised a poem of 200 lines. Its recitation gave complete instructions for delivering the perfect archery shot right from setting the bow, the placement of the legs, nocking the arrow, aiming, through to execution of the shot.

Novices began learning horsemanship by mounting swiftly in full armour over and over, and the *Furusiyya*, or art of cavalry warfare, manuscripts prescribe drills such as removing armour whilst riding, making tight turns, jumping and standing upon the saddle and stirrups and the study of the health and illnesses of horses, as well as the care of their tack. *Furusiyya* writings were also very specific on how the reins should be held, but this also extended to every piece of battle equipment, and to their balance: lance and dagger, sword and sling-shot, mace and javelin.

Shooting from the saddle was drilled and celebrated, all shooting was at the gallop and 100 per cent execution was required if a novice was to achieve the status of *Faris*. Studying and training in the science and art of warfare was the *raison d'etre* of a Mamluk. Even entertainment was centred on horsemanship and the *maydan*. This army of automatons was growing quickly under a new Sultan, and it was going to push the Crusader kingdom into the sea.

 ## The King of Jordan's Circassian Bodyguard. Distant blood brothers to the Mamluks of the Crusades era

The commander of the army should know the conditions of the fortress, the inaccessible places and those with ease of access, the impossible and possible places for military action. Further he should know the positions for mining the walls and for scaling ropes, siege ladders and grappling irons.

From a war manual written for Saladin by Al-Ansari.

Baybars was twice a regicide. He stabbed Qutuz in the back whilst the sultan was distracted by an accomplice making obeisance and kissing his hand during a hunting party in the desert. Baybars had enough support among the emirs to claim the state, and he recognised that jihad against the Crusaders would seal his hold on power. He installed a puppet caliph in Cairo, after a very cursory examination of his 'Abbasid' credentials, and he set the character of this army state. The Mamluk Sultanate would endure until 1517, and Baybars was its architect. The later Circassian Dynasty of the Sultanate still have a place in the Middle East as their descendants form the King of Jordan's personal bodyguard.

Baybars's jihad was more intricate, planned, ruthlessly executed and effective than that of any of the leaders before him. He had spies in European courts, he cultivated his relationship with the Genoese to undermine Latin unity, he made treaties with the Golden Horde to hem in Hulegu and he was systematic in his destruction of Outremer. Inland castles that were taken were refortified and garrisoned, while coastal strongholds were reduced to rubble to give no toehold for any Crusade that might be launched from Europe.

Baybars employed *wafidiyya*, essentially Turcoman warriors who had fled the Mongols in Persia and Anatolia, to constantly raid Crusader lands. Many Crusader lords gave up their leases on lands that they could not hope to defend, and the region to the south of the monastery on Mount Carmel was depopulated as farming there became impossible to maintain.

Baybars brought his Mamluk new model army first against Antioch. Bohemond VI's support of the Mongols and his close ties to Armenia, the Mongols' ally in the north, required that he be brought to heel. Raids began in 1261 and continued unabated. Hulegu had to station troops in the city just

to prevent its fall. In 1262 Saint Symeon was looted. Nazareth was the next to suffer. The city was plundered and the Church of the Virgin was levelled.

Caesarea fell after the Mamluks used makeshift rope ladders constructed from their bridles to haul themselves up the walls. Arsuf surrendered after its walls were flattened by siege engines and its immense moat was filled. The Templar castle of Safad soon went the same way.

The Mamluk cavalry would appear suddenly at the walls of a fortification. The attack would begin with a hail of arrows being fired at defenders, sometimes with Greek Fire, which would also be thrown using hand slings, then the light artillery of wheel-crossbows would be added, and then only a little later mangonels would be constructed and would begin bombardment. Sapping and filling-in of moats under cover of moveable shelters or *dabbaba* was also employed. Sieges were pressed rapidly and escalated against a constant and morale-sapping background of terrible thunder coming from the beating of huge paired drums carried on the backs of up to 300 camels. Mid-twelfth-century sources describe siege engines that could throw missiles of 80kg over an arrow's distance. Baybars possessed mangonels that hurled 400kg rocks at the walls of Crusader castles. It was beginning of the end.

 80 ## Mamluk Emirs' Blazons on Buildings in Jerusalem, on Metalwork, on Cairo Window Grills and Textiles; Enduring signs of the dynasty's obsession with rank and power.

When the investment is under way there should be no pause in the discharging of the mangonels against them and there should be no abating of the amount of mangonel fire in any hour of the day or night. To desist in attack against them is among that which cools their fright and strengthens their heart . . .

From a war manual written for Saladin by Al-Ansari.

Louis IX of France took the Cross once more in March 1267. He had also been corresponding with Abagha Khan, Hulegu's successor, for a joint attack on Syria and Egypt. Baybars had consolidated his rule over Syria well, and Mamluk governors were installed in all the major cities, where they left their mark in the shape of their blazons on the walls of their wards. Only Jaffa remained under Crusader control south of Acre. It was a potential landing point for a Crusader army and on 7 March Baybars appeared before its walls. A well-aimed mangonel missile killed three men standing close to Baybars as he planned the assault, but after only 12 hours of fighting the city fell. The city walls and the castle were demolished completely, in line with Mamluk coastal policy, and the marble decoration and wood of the structures were sent back to Cairo to become part of the sultan's new mosque.

The Templar castle of Beaufort was destroyed over a ten-day period by Baybars's vast siege engines, as the army moved onto Antioch. Flying columns of cavalry cut the city off from Saint Symeon and the Syrian Gates. Bohemond was not in the city and his constable made a foolhardy sortie against Baybars as his men were in the process of settling in for the siege. He was captured, and bombardments and assaults began immediately. On 18 May the Mamluks made a general attack on every sector of the walls; the garrison was stretched so thin that a break-in was inevitable, and it came on the Mount Silpius section of walls. There was a whole day of murder and rapine. The city gates were sealed to ensure that no citizen could escape.

Slaves and riches were distributed among the 'emirs of one hundred', Baybars's senior emirs, with which they could richly endow their 100 personal Mamluks, among the emirs of 40 and

down to the emirs of 10 and to the leading officers of the non-Mamluk troopers and infantry: Mamlukdom was a pyramid of interdependencies. Baybars also wrote to Bohemond of the sack:

If you had seen your churches destroyed, your crosses sawn asunder, the pages of the lying gospels exposed, if you had seen your enemy the Muslim trampling in the sanctuary, with the monk, the priest, the deacon sacrificed on the altar . . . the Churches of Saint Paul and Saint Peter pulled down and destroyed you would have said, 'Would to God that I was transformed to dust or would to God that I had not received the letter that tells me of this sad catastrophe . . .'

The Templars abandoned all their castles in the mountains surrounding Antioch, and north Syria slipped from Crusader control.

Antioch's first Crusader prince, the great Bohemond of Taranto, had taken the city in 1098 by cunning and it is to be wondered if these two men, the Norman adventurer and the slave soldier from the steppes, would not have had a grudging admiration for each other. Both were superb soldiers, both devious and charismatic, and both superb organisers of intelligence and vision.

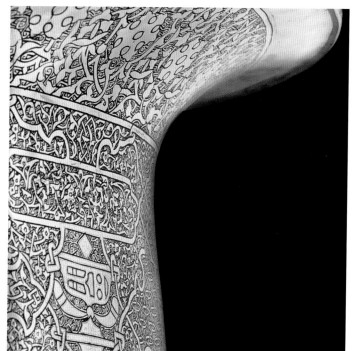

Walls Come Tumbling Down

81 **The Crown of Thorns, originally housed in Saint Chapelle, Saint Louis's purpose-built repository for the holy relic. Rescued from Notre Dame Cathedral during the blaze of 2019**

I turned around and saw the entire army of the Franj, *in combat formation. The interpreter said, 'the King reminds you not to forget the existence of this multitude of soldiers'.*

I replied. 'Well then, tell the King that there are fewer soldiers in his army than there are Frankish captives in the prisons of Cairo'.

The King nearly choked, then he brought the interview to a close; but he received us a short time later and concluded the truce.

Ibn Abd al-Zahir, an envoy of Baybars, relating a story of one of his missions to Acre.

Baybars made a secret pilgrimage to Mecca in 1269 and claimed guardianship over the Holy Cities. He also established trade relations with Sicily, first with Manfred, to whom he sent a giraffe and Mongol prisoners, and later with Sicily's new king, Charles of Anjou. Sicily's navy and strategic position made it a potential launch pad for any Crusade.

Charles's usurpation of the throne benefited Baybars as Charles's ambitions in Italy and his designs on Constantinople, now back in Byzantine hands, had frightened the Italian maritime republics to such an extent that they all rapidly made trade treaties with the sultan, who controlled Alexandria and the trade of India now that the Crusader ports were withering away.

These relationships became important in 1270 in the miring of King Louis IX's last Crusading venture. The Italians, who were to carry his army to the Levant, dragged their feet and the king's own brother, Charles of Anjou, appeared strangely reluctant to attack Egypt. The Crusade was eventually diverted to Tunis on the rather odd assumption that its ruler was converting to Christianity. It was a disaster. Pestilence did more damage to the Crusaders than the Muslim armies could ever have hoped to. King, later Saint, Louis died in Tunis of dysentery. His ventures had been largely unsuccessful but in 1248 he had obtained the Crown of Thorns which Baldwin II, the impecunious Latin Emperor of Constantinople, had hocked to the Venetians for 13,134 ducats, and so Louis's place in the lore of Crusading was secured.

Charles assumed command of the project and then abandoned it after securing trade agreements for Sicily from the Tunisians. Nothing was achieved for Outremer. Baybars then swiftly took the White Castle of the Templars and moved on to the great prize of Crak des Chevaliers, the immense Hospitaller castle that sat between Hama and Homs. The castle was encircled and despite heavy rain slowing down the bringing up of siege engines a brief but very effective barrage began. Crak, on an otherwise impenetrable mountain, had one accessible spur and the final assault was launched along

it after sappers brought down one of the massive towers on the outer wall. The Mamluks swarmed into the outer ring of defences and two weeks later they were able to force their way into the inner enclosure. There was a spirited defence by the knights but after ten days they capitulated and were given safe conduct to Tripoli.

Prince Edward of England arrived too late at Tunis but sailed on to Outremer with a small force. He began intriguing with the Ilkhan Abagha, but despite a feint into Syria by the Mongols, little came of this. It was however enough for Baybars to offer Acre a treaty, which was accepted, and then to order Edward's assassination.

Edward was stabbed by a poisoned dagger as he lay sleeping in his chamber. The wound was not fatal, but the prince lay near death for several months, and as soon as he was well enough he departed Outremer. Perhaps dealing with Baybars made an impression on the prince, since as Edward I of England he gained a reputation as being calculating and ruthless.

82 Mamluk-Style Quivers, their wide mouths and large capacity enabling rapid delivery of vast volumes of arrows

Father of the poor and miserable, killer of the unbelievers and the polytheists, reviver of justice among all.

An engraving on Mamluk armour.

The war with the Mongols had become a stalemate but the risk of an invasion that coincided with a Crusade remained. Baybars had long ago realised where the Mongols might be vulnerable; it was time

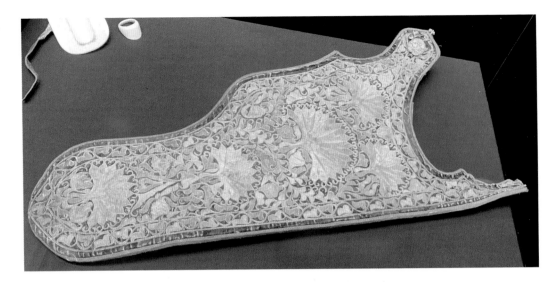

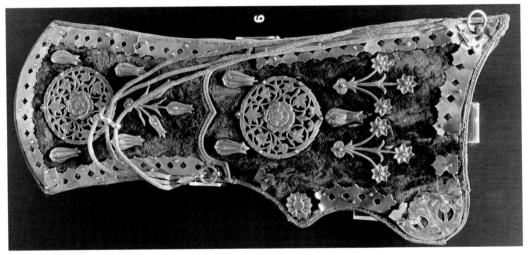

to make a play in Anatolia. Mongol control in the region was not strong and their puppet, the Pervane, had been secretly corresponding with the sultan since 1272. Mamluk raids and incursions began in 1274 from Aleppo into Anatolia as softening-up exercises and in 1275 Ayas, the main Ilkhanid port, was burnt and its inhabitants massacred.

In 1276 Baybars sent two Mamluk raids into Ilkhanate lands as a distraction, then he moved on Anatolia. Unfortunately the Anatolian princes started a rebellion against their Mongol overlords too early and Abagha sent 30,000 troopers to the Pervane along with a watchdog in the shape of General Tudawan. Many of the princes were caught and executed. Their organs were circulated around the province as a warning to others.

In February 1277 Baybars brought another army north. By April it was in the Taurus Mountains. A small force was sent ahead of the main army to reconnoitre. Methods of locating the enemy in mountainous terrain are discussed in *Furusiyya* treatises: the scout would take an empty wide-mouthed quiver, place it on the ground and then place his ear to its side to listen through this amplifier for the sound of hooves or

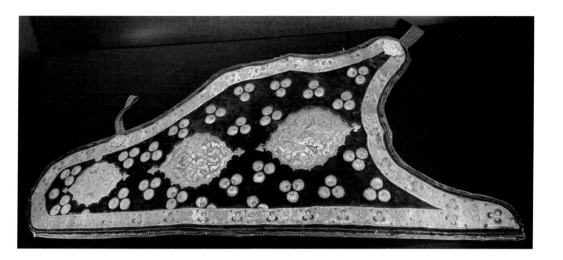

of marching feet. Perhaps this was how they detected the scouts of the Mongol army that led them to the garrison town of Abulustayn. The Mamluk army entered a plain next to the city at its south-east corner. The Mongols, along with their unwilling ally the Pervane, were at the south-west corner.

The Mongols crashed into the Mamluks and reached Baybars's *sanjaqiyya* or standard bearers. Baybars had been caught unprepared for once, and realising that if he lost his standards so far from home there would be panic among even his most battle-hardened troops, he rode with his bodyguard into the fray. The physical shock of the charge was enough to push the Mongols back and to relieve the centre, but the Mamluk left was also on the point of caving in. Baybars sent the army of Hama to the left and the battle was rebalanced. He then organised a counter-attack and the Mongols were pushed back.

The Mongols did not flee the field. They dismounted and many of them fought to the death. The Mamluks almost had to wade through the slaughter on their armoured horses but eventually they had slain enough of the brave Mongols to break their opponents' will to hold the field. The Pervane fled but the Mongol commander, Tudawan, was killed.

Once again the Mongols had been defeated by better soldiers. Mamluk high-volume or 'shower' shooting put down a much higher rate of fire than that of any other force in the medieval world. The Mamluk archer held several arrows, up to five, by the nock end between his palm and the last three fingers of his bow-drawing hand during firing so he did not reach to his quiver between each shot. Prester John would not be enough to save Outremer.

83 A Mamluk Mosque Lamp, decorated with the name of the patron who commissioned it, the emir Tankizbugha

Allah is the Light of the heavens and the earth. The similitude of His light is as a niche wherein is a lamp. The lamp is in a glass. The glass is as it were a shining star. . .

Quran Sura 24: Verse 35. *Al-Nur*, 'The Light'.

Baybars died on 1 July 1277 whilst in Damascus, at the age of about 50. He had ripped the Mamluk Sultanate from the hands of a man he had fought alongside and then murdered, but the state that he had acquired by this treacherous deed was an exhausted and frightened one. The state that he left behind was one that boasted a powerful well-organised army, secure borders, an efficient bureaucracy and a firm economic base. But he left his successors much more than that; he left them a model for them to follow. He created a bastion for the survival of Islamic culture, and artisans and scholars flocked to Mamluk Egypt from every part of the old Islamic world to create perfection in the arts of glassware, metalwork, textiles and architecture. His emblem, a red lion, is seen on numerous exquisite pieces. Patronage of the arts became de rigueur for any emir of high rank and the Qurans, metalwork, and mosque lamps of the Mamluk period are perhaps the finest of any ever produced.

Despite this, he himself was a stranger from the steppes, a barbarian from outside the Dar al-Islam whose chief entertainment was daily training in the military arts from noon until evening. He was enthroned by a caliph who hailed from a family that had been titular heads of the Islamic world for 500 years whilst he himself had no parents beyond his slave merchant and first master. He fought, even as sultan, under the yellow banners of the family of Saladin but he had killed, with his own hands, the last Ayyubid Sultan of Egypt. He was confident and brave in his dealings with his adversaries and in public, but it is reported that he slept poorly and suffered from dyspepsia and nightmares. He kept loyalty with his *khushdashiyya*, his 'brothers' from his days as a cadet, but he was cruel in the extreme to enemies. He was not, however, rage-driven like Abagha or Hulegu; for him

terror was a political instrument. He was king of the Egyptians but he married a daughter of the Khwarazmians and rarely spoke Arabic and was as much a Turkish warrior chief as an Islamic sultan. He rose by virtue of merit through a system that gave nothing by inheritance or by bloodline, but he tried, unsuccessfully, to secure the sultanate for his family's line. He was the champion of orthodox Sunni Islam but he kept his own Sufi, a religious mystic who predicted the fall of Crusader cities and who practised a form of Islam more akin to that of the steppes than to the cities of Egypt. He ruled from his war charger but his mausoleum in Damascus is now Syria's national library.

He was adept in international diplomacy but as likely to use assassination as negotiation. One version of his death has the sultan drinking from the wrong glass after flavouring its contents with poison meant for a minor Ayyubid emir. His biographer, al-Zahir, has it that, 'fortune made him king', but the sultan was in fact very much a self-made man.

84   A Mamluk Brass Bowl with Silver Inlay. The lotus, a motif brought from China by the Mamluks' deadliest enemies the Mongols, became almost ubiquitous in Islamic art after the thirteenth century

We send you the said messengers and ask you to send an expedition and army to the land of Egypt, and it shall be now that we from this side and you from your side shall crush it between us with good men; and that you send us by a good man where you wish the aforesaid done. The Saracens from the midst of us we shall lift and the lord Pope and the Great Khan Qubilai will be lords.

From a letter, still held in the Vatican, detailing the Ilkhan Arghun's strategy to destroy the Mamluk Sultanate by a simultaneous Crusade and Mongol invasion. It would never come to pass. Pope Honorius IV does not seem to have replied.

Baybars's son, Baraka, was swiftly deposed by a junta of senior emirs, and the Mamluk dynasty would often remain a one-generation monarchy despite the best efforts of sultans to place their offspring upon the throne.

Baraka's father in-law, the emir Qalavun, took power. Because of his extreme good looks he had acquired the nickname of al-Alfi, 'of one thousand', as this was the high price that had been paid for him in the slave market, whereas Baybars had been sold at a clearance price after being returned by his first master because of a cast or squint in his eye. Qalavun was also an impressive soldier and despite Baybars's intense mistrust of anyone who was not of his *khushdashiyya*, he had been a key confidante in the decision-making processes during the Mongol war. This said, the new sultan still

faced years of plots and dissent throughout Syria which had to be crushed city by city and emir by emir, and it was a senior emir's revolt in Damascus that brought the Mongols back to Syria. Qalavun had undertaken an almost Stalinist purge of the higher officers of the Mamluk military elite in an attempt to root out disloyalty, and he now faced the Ilkhan with an army which was far inferior to the one that Baybars had built.

Abagha Khan mustered a huge force of 120,000 troopers, and in the autumn of 1281 Qalavun had to scratch together an army which might just be capable of facing the storm. In Tripoli Crusaders donned Mongol helmets to try to convince the Mamluks that the Mongols were also landing there to force them to fight a two-front war.

Two battles took place in the early morning of 29 October. Qalavun had only about 30,000 men on the field but his army's line extended beyond that of the Mongols, the wings were made strong at the expense of the centre. Qalavun's fear was that the Mongols' numbers would simply roll up his flanks and envelop his army.

The Mongol right wing had immediate success and broke the Mamluk left. So convinced of victory were the men of this army that they sat down to rest on the side of Lake Homs. This was a mistake since as in the other battle the Mamluk right had withstood a series of Mongol charges and then counter-attacked, folding the Mongol left wing back onto the Mongol centre. At this point the Royal Mamluks advanced and started to strike standard bearers in the Mongol lines with superbly aimed arrows, a task for which they practised endlessly in the *maydan*. This assault on their communications caused chaos in the Mongol army, and its centre and left became one confused mass of men that struggled to clear the field under the hacking of Mamluk sabres and showers of arrows.

Then the Mongols that had been enjoying a lakeside sojourn returned and the sultan found himself alone. He hushed his battle drums and waited quietly until it dawned on his enemies that their compatriots were either dead or in flight. They fled the field, joining a retreat that soon became a death march. The Ilkhanate went through a virtual collapse, leaving the Mamluks a free hand against the Crusaders.

85 A Portal in Sultan al-Nasir's Mausoleum in Cairo. The arch was taken as booty from the Crusader church of Saint Jean in Acre by the Mamluks in 1291

The Franks shall not restore any wall, castle or tower of fortress, whether old or recent, outside the walls of the here places, Acre, Athlit and Sidon. If one of the Frankish maritime kings or others should move by sea with the intention of bringing harm to our lord the Sultan and his son in their territory to which this truce applies, the Lords of the kingdom and Masters in Acre are required to inform our Lord the Sultan and his son of their movement two months before their arrival in the Islamic territory covered by this truce . . .

From an accord between Qalavun and Acre, 1283.

Qalavun's victory had been a damned close-run thing and the presence of a Frankish enemy force in his rear, however small, could have swung the battle and thereby the war. Unfortunately, apart from a few renegade Hospitallers, the leaders of Outremer had tied their forces into pacts of neutrality with the Mamluks, hoping to survive by his clemency and not by armed help from the West.

The Hospitallers were punished for their presence at the Battle of Homs by the destruction of their castle of Margat in 1285. The maritime fort of Maraclea was sacrificed by the Crusaders when the sultan made its destruction the price of his withdrawal from Tripoli. In 1287 an earthquake levelled the walls of Lattakieh and the Mamluks walked into the city. In October 1287 Bohemond VII of Tripoli died and factions began to tear the city's unity apart. Qalavun had been intriguing with the Venetians against Bohemond and the Genoese in the city for some time and was only now prevented from finishing the city by the death of his favourite son. He finally took up a siege in 1289, and this briefly unified the Christians within the city's walls. Galleys under Venetian, Genoese and Pisan colours filled the harbour and supplied the city, and Louis IX's regiment from Acre and Cypriot knights joined the garrison. Tripoli could only be attacked via its narrow causeway. Qalavun lined up his catapults opposite the city to give covering fire, but it was hard going for his men, the thin neck of land made it hard to make their superior numbers tell, and the defenders could use all their forces on one small section of wall. The Mamluk artillery then concentrated on one spot, the south-east corner of the land walls. After a month, its towers disintegrated and the Venetian and Genoese ships in the harbour promptly raised anchor and sailed away from the doomed city. High-ranking Franks also took ship for Cyprus and abandoned the citizens. This desertion caused chaos inside Tripoli, and Qalavun ordered a general attack on 26 April. Every Christian man was killed and every woman or child was enslaved. Mamluks rode their horses as far as they could into the sea and then swam, whilst pulling their mounts along by the reins, to reach an island off Tripoli to slaughter its inhabitants.

Bohemond VII's bones were exhumed and strewn around the city. Tripoli's walls were levelled, in continuance of Baybars's scorched-earth policy for the coastline. Acre had to be next, but Qalavun knew its reduction would require a massive investment in siege engines. He renewed his truce with the city, but also built the largest mangonel ever seen in the Middle East: al-Mansura, 'the Victorious'. In 1290 a riot ensued in Acre after the seduction of a Christian wife by an Eastern merchant. Every bearded man that the mob could find was killed. Qalavun had his *casus belli* and he was ready. However, he died only five miles into the march. The task of finally removing the *Franj* from Syria would fall to his son, Khalil, about whom the sultan had once said, 'I will not set Khalil over the Muslims'.

Old Enemies, New Enemies

86 The Giostra in Arezzo, Italy. Twice a year, the knights of the Crusader Kingdom are remembered in a joust undertaken by competing quarters of the city against their old enemy, Il Saraceno

With these conquests all the lands of the coast were fully returned to the Muslims, a result undreamed of. Thus were the Franj, *who had once nearly conquered Damascus, Egypt and many other lands expelled from all Syria and the coastal zones. God grant that they never set foot there again!*

Abu'l Fida, a 19-year-old Ayyubid emir who fought with the Mamluks at Acre.

Saladin had used no more than ten mangonels at any siege; at the siege of Acre in 1291 the Mamluks deployed over ninety. In 1272 Persian engineers were employed by the Mongols to destroy the Chinese

fortress city of Xiangyang, which had been thought to be impregnable. The Mamluks had both the resources and the technology to bring down Acre's walls.

Khalil used his father's funeral to inflame the Egyptians' fervour for Holy War, before taking the army to Syria in March. *Ghazis* recruited in Damascus actually outnumbered regular army troopers. Men of the *ulama* helped to push the mangonels, but snow delayed the journey to Acre and oxen pulling the 100 carts of disassembled parts died of exposure.

Acre's garrison was bolstered by the arrival of troops from Cyprus, and the Hospitallers and Templars garrisoned in the city had strengthened the city's walls. Frankish ship-artillery in the harbour fired upon the right flank of the besieging army, until a storm wrecked many of them. The Crusaders also had the courage of desperation and Christian knights rode out daily to offer battle and single combat.

The bombardment of the city lasted six weeks. The Crusaders padded the walls with straw to dampen the missiles' impact, but the Mamluks fired these with incendiary arrows. Siege engines punched holes through walls and Mamluk infantry moved through the rubble. It was hard going. The bombardment was redoubled and sappers dug at every tower. The Crusaders burnt the Tower of King Hugh on 8 May as it was crumbling away beneath them. The Tower of the English then fell, along with Countess Blois's Tower. A section of wall above Saint Anthony's Gate then came down and with it the Tower of Henry II. The Mamluks charged through what was now a gaping hole in the outer walls, but were held at Saint Anthony's Gate, and denied entry to the city proper by a desperate stand from the Templars and Hospitallers.

On 17 May the Crusaders pleaded for a truce. This was refused, and the negotiations ended abruptly when the Crusaders attempted to kill the sultan with a well-aimed mangonel shot. Khalil ordered a general offensive to the continuous beating of drums. The defenders' heads were kept down by endless volleys of arrows and every part of the walls was assaulted. The Mamluks forced the Accursed Tower and then fought their way along the walls to secure Saint Anthony's Gate. The gate was opened and the troops flooded in. Within three hours *ghazi* banners were flying on every battlement.

One last tower held out. The sultan ordered it mined, and it collapsed, killing everyone inside. Meanwhile a brutal sack was being carried out in the city by the *ghazi* irregulars. Male inhabitants of the city were killed regardless of their faith, whilst women and children were taken for enslavement. Richer inhabitants could not escape as they had at Tripoli: they were tortured until they revealed where their gold and silver was hidden.

Khalil ordered the destruction of Acre's walls and then accepted the surrender of Saida, Beirut and Tyre. The war in the Holy Land was over, the Crusades were not.

An Anatolian Carpet with Animal Designs, c. fourteenth century

By the providence of God the city of Constantine again became subject to the Emperor of the Romans, in a just and fitting way, on the 25th July, in the fourth indiction, in the 6769th year since the creation of the world, after being held by the enemy for fifty-eight years.

The Byzantine historian George Akropolites writing of the quiet death of the Latin empire of Byzantium in 1261, and the return of the Greeks.

The Ilkhanate collapsed in 1336, and from the wreckage of the Mongol province of Anatolia a number of Turkish warlord statelets emerged. Byzantine aristocrats and their personal armies had returned to Europe upon the 'defeat' of the Latins, as the Empire concentrated its efforts on bringing the Black Sea coast and Bulgaria back to suzerainty, and on recovering the Peloponnese and the Morea. The emperor, Michael, also had to resist the rising Orthodox state of Serbia, and the ambitions of Charles of Anjou and of Sicily, and he briefly embraced Catholicism following the Council of Lyon in 1274 to gain assistance against Charles in Thessaly.

Byzantine military shortcomings required the employment of Turkish mercenaries in the army, and of the employment of *akritai*, nomad mercenary warriors, to defend the Anatolian border. The problem was that these nomads were highly attracted to successful 'Turkish' tribes from over the border. Such associations could be found across Eurasia from the times of Attila through to the times of Chinggis Khan. The tribes that operated in Anatolia contained Byzantine Greeks, Turks,

Kurds and Armenians. The most successful of these warrior bands were the Ottomans, and they also attracted Turks fleeing the disasters to the east. It was local success in the borderlands and against other local Turkish lords that brought more and more *akinji*, or raiders, to the standard of Osman.

Europe was pulled into Anatolian affairs by Turkish piracy, and the Venetians, along with Cypriot and Papal troops, took Smyrna in 1344 to deny its port to the pirate emirs. Then Anatolia came to Europe as a Byzantine civil war began between the regent, John Kantakouzenos, and the party of the infant emperor, John V Palaiologos. Kantakouzenos allied with Serbia in 1342 but the Serbian boyars soon enough double-crossed him and he turned to the Anatolian Turks for assistance. Ottoman troopers were carried across the Dardanelles by the small Byzantine navy and they quickly conquered Thrace, but Macedonia was lost to the Serbs. The Ottomans plundered Greece, and Bulgaria after its Tsar allied with the faction of John V. To add to Byzantium's torture, the Black Death ravaged Constantinople between 1346 and 1349.

Kantakouzenos took the throne, and the Ottoman sultan, Orhan, married his daughter. By 1352 20,000 Ottoman troops fought for Kantakouzenos against John V and his Serbian allies at the Battle of Demotika. The Ottomans gained more from their subsequent victory than Kantakouzenos, who eventually lost Constantinople to John. After conducting several campaigns in the service of Kantakouzenos Orhan politely presented a bill of expenses. It called, among other items, for the surrender to him of a Greek stronghold on the European side of the Dardanelles. Like many another foolish and ambitious schemer, the Greek discovered too late that it was easier to summon the Devil than to get rid of him. After vain remonstrances he was obliged to make over the small castle of Cimpe Tzympe to his Ottoman ally in 1354. The Ottomans were in Europe and Crusades would be launched again and again to try to dislodge them.

88 Statues of John of Matha, Felix of Valois and Saint Ivan on Charles Bridge, Prague. The work honours the founders of the Trinitarians, an order that redeemed Christians in captivity under the Turks, and Saint Ivan, the patron saint of the Slavs, 1714

Six centuries ago, Serbia heroically defended itself in the field of Kosovo, but it also defended Europe. Serbia was at that time the bastion that defended European culture, religion, and European society in general . . .
Speech given in 1989 by Slobodan Milošević, at the Gazimestan monument on the Kosovo field, commemorating the 600th anniversary of the Battle of Kosovo. The stoking of ethnic tension between Serbs and Albanians in Kosovo was the Serbian president's clear intent.

By 1363 the Ottomans were impinging on regions claimed by Serbia, Bulgaria and Hungary, and a coalition army under Louis I of Hungary challenged the new Ottoman Sultan Murad I's army near Adrianople. It was destroyed in short order on the banks of the Maritsa River. The

venture had a papal blessing but was not called as a Crusade. In 1371 the Serbs and Bulgarians tried again to take Adrianople, now renamed Edirne and the Ottoman capital. The Christian army was annihilated, again on the Maritsa River. Such was the magnitude of slaughter that the Ottomans referred to the battle as the 'Destruction of the Serbs'.

Bulgaria began to fall apart under Ottoman raids and the sultan's armies entered Albania and captured the city of Nis. Serbia disintegrated as a buffer against the Turks and in many ways the second battle of Maritsa was far more significant than the more famous first battle of Kosovo in 1389. The Ottomans also began to enslave women and young Christian boys:

They harvested the young men. They took one in every five prisoners captured in the raids and delivered him to the Porte. They then gave these young men to the Turks in the provinces so that they should learn Turkish, and then they sent them to Anatolia. After a few years they brought them to the Porte, and gave them the name Yeni Ceri. Their origin goes back to this time . . .

These *Yeni Ceri*, 'new men', were of course the Janissaries and their rigidly disciplined regiments took Sofia and made Constantinople a captive island in a Turkish sea. Sultan Murad took forces from his new Serbian vassals to campaign in Anatolia, and the Serb heavy cavalry with its composite bows, maces and horse-armour was particularly effective against the Ottomans' Turkish enemies.

In Serbia, Prince Lazar took the opportunity of Murad's absence to form a union of Serbian, Macedonian and Montenegrin nobles. He maintained his vassalage to the sultan but continued to conspire against him. In 1389 he challenged the Ottomans as Murad had again been forced to campaign in Anatolia. Unfortunately for Lazar, Murad returned to the Balkan theatre with incredible rapidity. The battle took place on Kosovo Polje, 'the Field of Blackbirds'. Both Murad and Lazar were killed, and the battle ended as a vicious, bloody draw. What turned it into an Ottoman victory was the collapse of the Serbian nobles' resistance after the battle. Virtually all the boyars took vassalage under the new sultan, Bayezid.

A Crusade against the Turks was called after Bayezid reportedly claimed that he intended to conquer Hungary and Italy and to water his horse in the altar of Saint Peter's. Both Boniface

X, the Pope in Rome, and his rival Benedict VIII, the Antipope in Avignon, supported the venture and by September 1396 a force comprised of Hungarians, French knights and troops and contingents from the Holy Roman Empire had reached the city of Nicopolis after a march from Buda and a crossing of the Danube River that took some eight days. Those doughty Crusader enemies of the Muslims, the Knights Hospitallers, also sent a detachment from their new home of Rhodes.

89 The Chapel of the Holy Cross, Karlstejn, Czech Republic. Emperor Charles IV created the room to represent the New Jerusalem described in Revelation 21, c. 1350

Constantinople will be taken, once this city is taken the Franks will be obliged to fight the barbarians in Italy and on the Rhine.

> The Byzantine Emperor's chief adviser, Demetrios Kydones, following negotiations with the papacy that failed to bring direct aid to Constantinople.

As discussed earlier, there was now an established view among Western European Catholics that they held Jerusalem within themselves, so the Crusade of Nicopolis was a defence of Christendom for sure. However, this Crusade, and the others that would follow it were not to bring succour to Eastern Christians but rather, as Phillipe de Mezieres's fourteenth-century Crusade treatise stated, 'to spread Catholicism to the eastern countries'.

The Crusader army added Bulgarian and Wallachian allies during its march to bring its strength up to 16,000 men. Nicopolis's governor was certain that Bayezid would come to his aid and was prepared to resist the Crusaders to the utmost. The Crusaders boasted no siege engines. Bayezid marched from Edirne and met up with his Serbian vassals.

Divisions appeared among the Christian leaders in a war council. A plan for mounted archers to meet the Ottoman vanguard and dispatch the skirmishers before the heavily-armed French knights rode into meet the Janissary infantry and regular Ottoman troops whilst the Hungarians protected their flanks from the Turkish cavalry was presented by King Sigismund of Hungary. This was rejected out of hand by the French nobles. They stated that they would ride at the Ottomans head on and be the first to engage the enemy. With his allies evidently set on a death-or-glory charge Sigismund had little else to do except to organise his own army's battle plan. Word then came that the sultan's army was only six hours march away and this apparently caused confusion in the Crusader camp.

The French vanguard charged the Ottomans who were still deploying around Nicopolis. Sigismund's Hungarians along with Hospitaller Knights, Germans and other allies were formed up as a second wave. There was initial success as the French cut through the Janissaries. Ottoman archery and rows of sharpened stakes among the Ottoman positions took down a considerable portion of the French

cavalry but the Ottoman line was broken. The French pursued stragglers even though this meant an uphill ride for those still mounted and an exhausting trudge for the half of the force that had lost its horses but remained in heavy armour. At the top of the slope the French then found themselves faced by a corps of Turkish and Serbian cavalry that Bayezid had concealed among the ravines. During a pell-mell retreat the Wallachians and Transylvanians deserted. Sigismund and his Hungarians were, however, nearly able to turn defeat into victory as they pushed the Turkish cavalry from the field, but then the Serbian troopers entered the conflict with '15,000 men and many bannerets' and overwhelmed them.

Sigismund managed to escape via a fisherman's boat. France had lost much, Hungary more, but even the victor, Bayezid, was distressed by the degree of slaughter his army had suffered in the battle. On the morning of 26 September the sultan ordered an assembly of the French and Hungarian prisoners and after separating the chief nobles from the rest he forced them to watch the execution of up to 3,000 captives, an act that took until late afternoon to complete.

A Ceremonial Sword of the Order of the Dragon, a Catholic order created by Sigismund of Hungary in 1408. Its members swore to combat heretics and the Ottomans

Ah, fair Zabina! we have lost the field; And never had the Turkish emperor
So great a foil by any foreign foe. Now will the Christian miscreants be glad,
Ringing with joy their superstitious bells, And making bonfires for my overthrow . . .
Tamburlaine the Great Part One, Act III, Scene III. The Sultan Bayezid following
his capture at the Battle of Ankara.

Following the Battle of Nicopolis Bulgaria was completely subsumed into the Ottoman Empire and ceased to exist. Bayezid raided Hungary, Wallachia, and Bosnia and the Albanian nobles all accepted vassalage under him. Constantinople was also besieged again until Manuel II agreed that the House of Osman would confirm all future Byzantine emperors.

Constantinople would have fallen to Bayezid in 1402, but it was saved by the last great eruption of the Mongol hordes. Timur Leng claimed the heritage of Chinggis Khan through marriage, and this brilliant but brutal generalissimo campaigned in the Middle East in 1399. Bayezid attempted to ally with the Mamluk Sultanate but Timur was able to rapidly destroy the Mamluk army of Syria at Aleppo and then moved on to Baghdad, where he built 120 towers of skulls from its slaughtered inhabitants and reddened the Tigris with their blood.

Timur moved on Ankara and Bayezid's troops arrived in poor order after a forced march. The Battle of Ankara was the greatest battle that Timur had yet fought. Bayezid's Asian levies mutinied and only the Serbs and the Janissaries kept the Ottoman army from complete destruction. Bayezid was captured. He died in captivity a year later, and it appeared that the Ottoman Empire was at an end. It was saved by Timur's death whilst campaigning in China. Bayezid's sons fought a protracted civil war amongst themselves but the empire survived.

Mehemmed eventually defeated his brothers and Wallachia fell to the renascent Ottomans. In 1422 Constantinople was besieged again. The Christians were in retreat everywhere, and the Order of the Dragon had been formed as a response to the losses. Its most famous adherent, the Hungarian lord Jonas Hunyadi, led a tenacious resistance in the early 1440s, and even managed to secure a peace on reasonably equal terms with Sultan Murad II in 1444 after three years of constant war. He used techniques that in many ways sat against established 'chivalric' warfare. He depended heavily on infantry, handgunners, cannon, and war wagons to form laagers from within which his men could stymie the charges of the Turkish *sipahi* cavalry, and behind which his heavy cavalry could form up to charge the Ottoman positions. Hunyadi would end his days as an *Athletae Christi* for his efforts defending Christendom. The honour would also be bestowed on the Albanian, George Skanderbeg.

Skanderbeg had been sent to the Ottoman court in 1423 as a noble hostage for his father's good conduct. He underwent military training in Edirne, converted to Islam and took Iskander Bey as his Muslim name. In 1443 he deserted the Ottoman army and led 300 Albanian troops away with him. He formed a league with minor Albanian lords and defeated the Ottoman pasha's army of some 25,000 men with only 7,000 infantry and 8,000 cavalry through the very unchivalrous method of hiding half his cavalry in a forest, which then swooped into the battle and closed it. The Ottoman losses may have been as great as 10,000 killed or captured. Skanderbeg would go on to torment his foes with a long campaign of guerrilla warfare, and to also undertake pitched battles against tremendous odds.

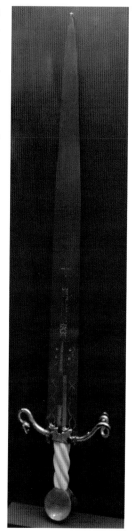

The Slow Death of Chivalry

91 Fifteenth-century War Wagons were decidedly unheroic and stood against all notions of chivalry, but they afforded vital protection for infantry and handgunners against cavalry and could also transport artillery shot and other tools of 'modern war'

May Allah never grant me another such victory.

The Ottoman Sultan Murad II on the battlefield, having just defeated the Crusade of Varna in 1444.

Hunyadi's successes sent the papacy into a frenzy of diplomacy and preaching to push the Turks from Europe. At the Hungarian diet in April 1444 a grand coalition was formed under Vladislaus III, King of Poland and Hungary, though under the tutelage of Hunyadi. The plan was complex. The Crusader army would follow the Danube, and Burgundian, Venetian and Genoese ships were to close the straits and deny the Turks reinforcements from Anatolia. The Greeks were expected to make diversionary attacks in the Peloponnese. In a flight of fantasy the Crusade looked beyond freeing Varna and on to liberating Jerusalem.

Many Serbian and Hungarian nobles had received favourable terms from Murad in 1443 and refused to participate. However, the timing of the Crusade was propitious; there were Janissary pay riots, successful uprisings in Albania led by the rebel Skanderbeg, and Murad had 'retired', possibly exhausted by the horrors of the battlefield.

At Varna the Crusaders found a massive Ottoman army waiting for them. The Venetian-Burgundian fleet had failed to close the Dardanelles and the Genoese transported Murad II, who had come out of retirement, and his reserves across to Europe. Byzantium simply stood aside.

Hunyadi took the centre with about 3,000 men comprising the king's bodyguard, and Hungarian mercenaries and nobles. The left of the Hungarian line was comprised of about 5,000 Transylvanian troops and German mercenaries. On the right 6,000 German Crusaders were under the command of the Bishop of Varadin and Cardinal Cesarini.

Murad had 20,000 cavalry on his right, another 15,000 on his left and his centre was comprised of some 10,000 Janissaries and other infantry levies, well dug in and behind barricades on a small hill. He pinned the peace treaty of 1443 above his tent as evidence of the Hungarians' perfidy.

A sudden wind blew up and knocked down all of the Christian banners except that of Vladislaus and then Murad began his attack on the left. The Crusader right plunged into the attacking Ottomans, exposing the centre's flank, and Murad then sent his right wing of cavalry against the Hungarian left but Hunyadi countered this with an attack he personally led against the Ottoman right from the centre. The Hungarians seemed to be winning the battle at this point, but their right wing was in fact near collapse and only a few of the troops made it back to the safety of the war-wagon laager before the rout.

Hunyadi's energy and bravery still nearly won the battle. He led part of the Hungarian left and centre across the battlefield to attack the Ottoman left. The Royal Guards joined him and the Ottoman cavalry broke. Murad II had only his Janissaries and infantry levies left on the field. Victory was snatched away from Hunyadi by Vladislaus. Hunyadi had warned the king to wait for the whole army to reform before engaging the Ottoman centre, but Vladislaus was swayed by nobles who were jealous of Hunyadi's reputation and who wanted their sovereign to claim the victory. The Janissaries' hail of arrows destroyed his cavalry and killed Vladislaus. The Crusader army fled the field but the Ottoman army was so broken that it could not pursue them.

Tombstones of Heretics: Bogomils in Bosnia and Cathars in Carcassonne, thirteenth century

To corrupt the faith, whereby the soul lives, is much graver than to counterfeit money, which supports temporal life. Since forgers and other malefactors are summarily condemned to death by the civil authorities, with much more reason may heretics as soon as they are convicted of heresy be not only excommunicated, but also justly be put to death . . .

Cut off the decayed flesh, expel the mangy sheep from the fold, lest the whole house . . . the whole body, the whole flock burn, perish, rot, die. Arius was but a single spark in Alexandria, but as it was not at once put out, the whole world was laid waste by his flame . . .

> Saint Thomas Aquinas writing, and quoting Saint Jerome,
> on the dangers of heretics to the body of the Catholic faith.

The Albigensian heresy of Languedoc had its origins in the Bogomil heresy of Bulgaria. The term Bogomil, freely translated, means 'dear to God'. The Bogomils were far beyond the pale for both the Orthodox and Catholic Churches, and this may well have had more to do with their antipathy for ecclesiastical hierarchy and their resistance to both state and church authorities than their actual beliefs, which were also certainly heretical. They believed in dualism and the creation of the world not by God, but by the Devil. Bogomils refused to pay taxes, to work in serfdom, or to fight in conquering wars. They disdained feudal society and the established churches as these were manifestations of Satan's creation. Both the Catholic and Orthodox Churches were alarmed by the apparent popularity of the creed among the lower orders. It spread in various forms across the Balkans, through to the Russian lands, and to Italy and France, where it evolved into Catharism.

Many times the Bogomils of the Balkans were threatened with extermination by the Church and by orders such as the Order of the Dragon who we met fighting the Turks in the last chapter, but the sect survived into the Ottoman period, despite the Hungarian kings using its existence as a consistent reason for 'crusading' against Bosnian lords and nipping away at their territory, and the pope despatching Franciscans to begin an Inquisition in Bosnia in 1291.

In Southern France no such lukewarm a resolution to heresy was contemplated, and a complete annihilation of the Cathars was undertaken over a period of 20 years from 1209 with the recruitment of 10,000 Crusaders from northern France and England, who attacked Montpellier, Carcassonne and Béziers. Almost the entire population of Béziers was slaughtered indiscriminately. The possibly apocryphal words of Amalric, a leader of the Crusade, 'Kill them all! God will know his own!' led to the killing of both Cathars and Catholics, and of nearly every man, woman and child in the city.

More blood and murder followed at Minerve, where many 'perfects', the leaders of the Cathar community, were given the option of conversion and to be identified by the wearing of a large yellow cross for the rest of their life, or burning at the stake. Three ladies did recant, but 140 'perfects' were burned. More than few walked into the flames willingly.

Toulouse was the next city to be tortured after their protector the Crusader King of Aragon, and hero of the *Reconquista*, Peter was killed in battle but the Cathar cities revolted and in 1225 the French crown had to directly intervene. Louis XIII led a Crusader army of a size far exceeding that of 1209 to Languedoc. Still, it was hard going, but the war was concluded by treaty in 1229.

The Crusade was followed by an Inquisition in 1234 that extinguished the sect. Whilst Saint Thomas perhaps gives us some indication of the motivations for the Crusade, there can also be no doubt that the Ile-de-France saw the south of the country as desirable and too independent. In some respects the Albigensian Crusade looks more like an invasion and land grab than a religious act.

93 Eisenstein's 1938 film *Alexander Nevsky,* in which Teutonic Knights are equated with the contemporary Nazi state of Germany, and the invading German armies of 1914. The presence of coal-scuttle helmets on the Crusader infantry and swastikas on the mitres of the Catholic bishops drove home the message of colonial feudalism being defeated by Russian folk heroes

Root out the era of paganism and spread the bounds of the Christian faith . . . fight in this battle of the war bravely and strongly like an active Knight of Christ . . .

A letter from Pope Innocent III to King Valdemar II of Denmark in 1209.

The Livonian Crusade in the Baltic region was a creation of the Archbishop of Bremen rather than the papacy, in a classic case of the tail wagging the dog. The archbishop saw a chance to extend

his province, and the papacy obligingly granted indulgences to those who crusaded in the service of the Livonian church. A certain Albert of Buxtehude was appointed as leader of the venture, and he would dominate the Baltics from 1198 to the 1230s. He used a technique, not unheard of in the twentieth and twenty-first century, of settling peasants from the Netherlands and Westphalia in lands east of Germany and then calling for a Crusade to protect these settlements once they were attacked by their pagan neighbours. Albert was given papal authority to recruit priests who had vowed to go to Jerusalem to work on his mission instead. A cult, 'Our Lady of Riga', developed over time that recruited pilgrims from Germany to campaign every summer. The military orders of the Teutonic

Knights and the Sword Brothers kept the front line intact during the winter. The Danes also exploited the perpetual Crusade's *Drang nach Osten*, or 'Drive to the East' to conquer the Pomeranian coast, and their fleets attacked Finland in 1191, Estonia in 1194, and Prussia in 1210. Valdemar II was competing with the Germans and the Swedes for these lands. His naval power in the Baltic Sea forced his fellow Crusaders to agree to his control of the new colonies even though its colonists were predominately German.

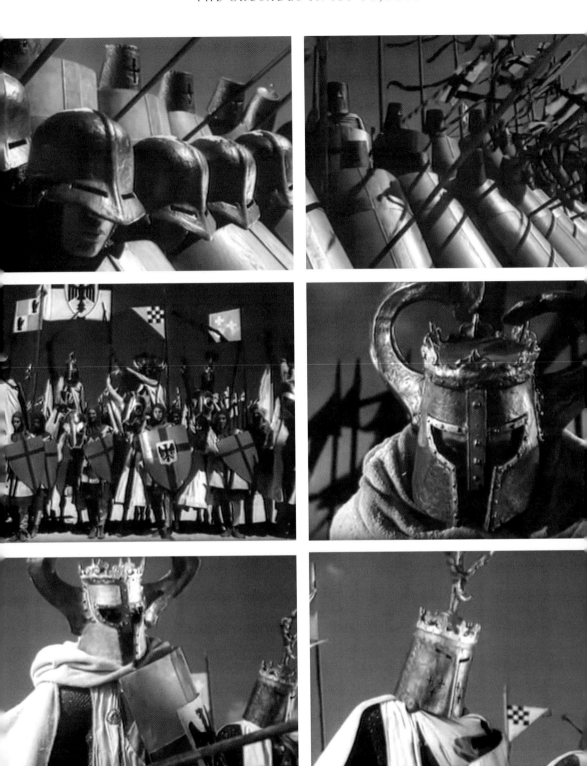

Under the leadership of the German Teutonic Knights the features of the perpetual Baltic Crusade became an ideology. A planned process of colonisation of each area, and the creation of trade points based on the city of Magdeburg's quarters, gates and tariffs was established. In many ways this connected the new towns of the East with the maturing trade system of the Holy Roman Empire and beyond, but the success of the venture hinged on the proximity of the leaders of this Crusade to the papacy. Unlike their opposite numbers in the Temple and Hospitaller Orders, the Teutonic Knights could always be confident of a Pope, such as Innocent III's, support:

We concede the same indulgence and privileges that are granted to those going to Jerusalem to all in Germany who in response to the appeals of the Teutonic Knights and without public preaching put on the sign of the Cross . . .

In 1283 Prussia, which had been at least half-converted to Catholicism, was made a wilderness by the Order, and its population was reduced to the status of serfdom in a brutal put-down of a revolt.

Of course, there were occasional setbacks. In 1242 Alexander Nevsky, the Grand Prince of Kiev, drew the Teutonic Knights onto the frozen Lake Teploe. After absorbing the initial shock of the Knights' charge, Alexander outflanked them on both the right and the left. The Crusaders exhausted themselves slipping on the ice and one final charge was enough to send them into a panicked retreat. That the knights drowned after the ice broke beneath them seems to have been a creation of Eisenstein.

94 The Cathedral of Saint Mary of the See, Seville. Its bell tower 'La Giralda', is a minaret built by the Almohad caliph Abu Yaqub Yusuf in 1198 for his grand mosque, with later Christian additions

I dare to imagine that, as the least of his exploits, entire kingdoms will fall beneath his laws; and my fond love is already persuaded that I behold him seated on the throne of Granada, the vanquished Moors trembling while paying him homage.

The Infanta from Corneille's *El Cid*.

The *Reconquista* predated the Crusades, and knights fighting in Spain received indulgences equal to those who battled for Jerusalem. The title of the venture is also something of a misnomer, as most of the knights who would eventually take Spain from the Muslims came from Navarre and beyond, and there was certainly a great deal of rubbing along with Muslim neighbours and short-term alliances between Christians and Muslims for quick gains. However, in response to a heavy defeat at Alarcos in 1195, Alfonso VIII of Castile received Crusade privileges from Pope Innocent III and by 1210 Alfonso had renewed the offensive and he pushed into Muslim territories. His success led to a further call for Crusade in 1212 in both France and Spain, and in Rome fasting and special prayers were ordered for a Christian victory. The response was strong in southern France amongst knights already engaged on the Albigensian Crusade and a large army mustered at Toledo. At the Battle of Las Navas de Tolosa the Muslims were routed after an heroic charge was led by Alfonso. Many Muslim castles immediately surrendered, and Andalucía was opened up to invasion. This was a turning point but a long, grinding campaign still lay ahead and the Papacy consistently fretted that the reconquest should not divert resources from Crusades to the Holy Land.

By the middle of the thirteenth century there was far more unified, concerted and powerful action, and Crusade privileges were given in 1229 for James I of Aragon and his expedition to the Balearics,

and military orders specific to the Iberian Peninsula evolved. By 1248 only Granada remained to be taken in Spain by the *Reconquista*, as Seville fell in that year, and Cordoba had surrendered in 1236. Portugal was completely Christian-controlled by 1250.

But then for nearly a century the pace of reconquest slowed as the Marinids of Morocco fought to preserve Moorish Andalucía. They may have seen it as a buffer, as a Crusade was being preached to invade Africa. Alfonso X of Castile tried to recruit King Henry III of England and King Hakon of Norway for the venture, but in 1264 he had to face a large-scale Muslim revolt alone and he expelled all Muslims from Murcia. Granada survived with Marinid support, and the long war would continue with Crusades bringing warriors to Spain from England, Bohemia, France and Germany. However, Gibraltar remained a Muslim possession allowing entrance to the campaign for Marinid troops,

and Alfonso XI died of the Black Death while besieging it in 1350. The reconquest then went dormant for nearly a century with the Christians unable to subjugate Granada and the Muslims unable to attempt any significant onslaught.

The union of Aragon and Castile in 1479 reinvigorated the war. Indulgences were promulgated and the completion of conquest was widely seen as a compensation for the loss of Constantinople. Malaga was taken in 1487 and a permanent fortress-town, Santa Fe, was constructed next to Granada to demoralise and to dominate the Muslim defenders. The final surrender came in January 1492. Rome was illuminated with torches and bonfires and bullfights were organised by Cardinal Rodrigo Borgia.

95 The Hussite Warlord Jan Žižka on Vítkov Hill in Prague. Planned in 1937, completed in 1950

Ye who are God's warriors and of his law, Pray to God for help and have faith in Him;
That always with Him you will be victorious.
Christ is worth all your sacrifices, He will pay you back a hundredfold.
If you give up your life for Him you will receive eternal life.
Happy is he who dies fighting for the truth.

The Hussite Battle Hymn, sung as late as 1937 at the funeral
of the Czechoslovak President, Masaryk

As a response to the siege of Constantinople in 1422 Pope Martin tried to form a league between Crusaders and the Italian republics. This was hampered by the Hussite heresy's emergence in Bohemia. Jan Hus, strongly influenced by the English Wycliffites, had attacked sinful clergy and the privileged positions of German lords in the Czech lands. He was burned in 1415 but the Hussites took control of Prague and a war of words as well as a very bloody conflict on the ground ensued. Polemical verses such as the allegorical *Hádání Prahy s Kutnou Horou*, which presented Prague in the form of a lovely lady, symbolising the Hussites, battling the ugly hag of the Catholic city of Kutná Hora circulated and were answered by violence. The German miners of Kutná Hora tortured Hussites and flung them alive into the shafts of their mines. Indeed, so popular was the 'sport' that Catholic barons from across Bohemia could sell Hussite prisoners to the miners.

Sigismund, the Holy Roman Emperor, proclaimed that he would 'shit in the faces of the Hussites', and a markedly more intellectual argument was prepared by Pope Martin who called a universal Crusade against all heretics. It was proclaimed in March 1420 at an imperial diet in Wrocław. Sigismund took an army to Prague in early July comprised of Germans, Austrians and Hungarians and surrounded the city on three sides. The Hussites sat atop the long, narrow Vitkov Hill which dominated access to Prague from the East.

Sigismund moved on the hill late in the afternoon with a strong cavalry force. His opponent, the wily Jan Žižka, fortified the hill with ditches, blockhouses and walls built by peasant followers of the faith. Women joined the defenders of the hill, one of who was heard to shout 'Rather death than the Antichrist!' and though the Crusaders crossed the first and second ditches without difficulty they stalled when faced by infantry with pitchforks and flails. As the cavalry charge faltered Žižka attacked with a small group of his men and deployed crossbowmen to trap the Crusaders between them and the blockhouses. Behind the first wave more Crusader cavalry came up the hill, but they only made the situation worse for the knights trapped on the narrow ridge. As night came on the Crusaders tried to disengage themselves by riding to the steep cliff on the northern side of the hill and many of them were killed in the fall, while others tried to escape on the more gentle eastern slope and across the river but drowned in the attempt. A thousand Hussites, many of them peasants, had defeated an army of 20,000 Crusaders. Sigismund withdrew

to his tent and gave no further orders. Vitkov Hill was commonly referred to as Žižka's Hill from that day on.

The dominance of the knight on the battlefield was over. Battles of attrition won by crossbows, gunpowder and war wagons, such as those that the Hussites would deploy at the Battle of Německý Brod (now Havlíčkův Brod), were the future. Perhaps the nobles knew this from as long ago as 1139 when a Lateran Council had denounced the crossbow 'as being hateful to god'.

96 Vast Mosques and Extensions to the Body of Hagia Sophia. Ottoman contributions to the greatest city of the medieval age

How is the Greek church, so afflicted and persecuted, to return to ecclesiastical union and a devotion for the Apostolic See when she sees in the Latins only an example of perdition and the works of darkness, so that with reason she already detest them more than dogs?

Pope Innocent III.

Mehemmed II, who had failed to control the army and state in the 1440s, requiring Murad's resumption to the throne, was much more in control by 1452, and he recognised that taking Constantinople, the prize that had eluded the Muslims for centuries, would cement his reign. The West realized, far too late, that 'this time' the Ottomans were not going to turn back from conquering the city. Cardinal Isidore arrived in Constantinople in November 1452 with Venetian troops but also brought the pope's requirement that the great schism be healed by Constantine XI's acceptance of Catholicism before any assistance could be expected. A service dedicated to the union was therefore made in Hagia Sophia in December 1452 and the heads of the Orthodox Church agreed to the ending of the schism. They could not, however, carry the lower clergy and laypeople with them and widespread rioting followed the service. Genoa had even more to lose than Venice if Constantinople fell as Caffa, their Black Sea port, could be strangled by whoever controlled Constantinople. Two galleys and 700 troops were sent.

Byzantium's walls were not capable of resisting cannonballs and there were few emplacements for cannon. The famous floating chain that closed the Golden Horn was still extant and functional however, and the city boasted orchards, fresh water, and farm animals. Fish could also be landed daily from safe harbours and there was abundant water storage in the city. Mehemmed knew, therefore, that he would need to batter, not starve, the city into surrender.

The chain of the Golden Horn repelled the Ottoman navy, so Mehemmed constructed a long wooden slipway. The ships were taken overland and launched beyond the boom. Meanwhile the Ottoman guns, including the monster *Basiliske* had breached the walls at the gate of Saint Romanus. A series of night attacks failed, as did mining of the Blachernae Walls.

Ottoman engineers constructed a bridge across the Golden Horn to allow a swifter deployment of their forces as Mehemmed, nearly at the end of his resources and facing a coup by his emirs, prepared to gamble on a mass attack.

Despite lashing rain, sappers started to fill the defensive ditches around Constantinople in the early hours of 29 May. Three hours before dawn the artillery started up and an infantry attack began.

This first wave was virtually slaughtered. Ottoman ships then attempted to place scaling ladders against the walls but were repulsed. A further infantry assault failed at the Saint Romanus Gate.

Mehemmed had one more card to play, his 3,000 Palace Janissaries. After an hour fighting at the Romanus Gate they discovered a wall-gate had been left open after a Byzantine sortie. They managed to get their banner up on the battlements, this and the fatal wounding of the Genoese captain, Giustiniani Longo, caused panic in the defenders. The Venetians and Genoese bolted to their ships in the harbour, and Mehemmed poured troops into the breach.

Emperor Constantine, according to legend, died crying out heroically for a Christian among the Turks to take his head, but was more likely killed in the sack that had begun as soon as the defenders scattered from the walls.

The Sacro Monte of Varallo, Italy. Started in 1491 and added to until the seventeenth century, so that those, 'who could not go on a pilgrimage might see Jerusalem'

La grande aquila é morta!

'The Great eagle is dead!' A jubilant cry heard all over Venice along with the peals of church bells as the citizens of Europe heard of the death of Mehemmed II.

The establishment of Varallo and other pilgrimage sites across Europe was a direct result of the Turkish successes in southern Europe and the eastern Mediterranean. The Holy Land was beyond saving and even peaceful pilgrimage to Jerusalem was impossible. The Sacro Monte was begun by the Franciscan Bernardino Caimi, who had been a rector of the Palestinian Holy Places.

In some ways the fall of Constantinople was a sideshow, though it completed the process of centralisation of power in the Ottoman state under the sultan and away from the tribal elements of Anatolia. The main feature of the period was the gobbling up by the Turkish crocodile of territory and vassals and the challenge to the legitimacy of the German Emperor by the new possessors of the throne of the Byzantine Emperors, who had been, after all, the equal of the Apostles.

1448 saw the second Battle of Kosovo. Hunyadi announced it as a Crusade and demanded Serbian participation but the campaign was never papally endorsed with indulgences or preaching. The battle lasted for three days but the body count for Hunyadi's defeated Hungarians was far lower than would be expected. This was because there were wagonbergs, fortified infantry lines with handgunners and artillery. The cavalry were pushed to the wings for flanking manoeuvres and not chivalric all-or-nothing charges. Attrition and protection of the army was the new ethos.

In 1456 Hunyadi defeated the Ottomans at the siege of Belgrade with professional troops and armed peasants. The defence of the city on the Danube was close to being a Crusade, as John of Capistrano recruited a people's army through preaching by priests and monks across Hungary, Serbia and the Holy Roman Empire. Capistrano preached, 'God wills it that we chase the Turks out of Europe and for whosoever follows me, I will obtain plenary indulgence for him and his family!' His Crusaders were armed, in the main, only with slings and clubs, and there was no illusion about conquering Jerusalem or retaking Constantinople. These men fought for hearth, home and the preservation of Christendom. Both Hunyadi and Capistrano died in Belgrade of plague after their victory.

Mehemmed faced other peasant armies under the Transylvanian Vlad Dracula, Stephen the Great of Moldova, who handed out a severe beating to the Ottomans at the Battle of Vaslui, and from the tireless Skanderbeg, but still Mehemmed's juggernaut rolled on. In 1480 he made an amphibious invasion of Otranto in Italy.

There was relief at the death of Mehemmed and the rule of Bayezid II was dominated by the danger of his fugitive brother, Cem, who was the long-term guest of the Vatican, and the Janissaries who acted very much as kingmakers and restrained the powers of the sultan. This said, during his reign Bayezid brought Moldova to vassalage, and Skanderbeg died of malaria in 1468. When the Ottomans later captured the town that housed Skanderbeg's tomb, they opened it, not to desecrate it, but to take fragments of his bones for amulets that they hoped would bring them the same martial valour that he had always displayed.

A Salt Cellar with Portuguese Soldiers and a Caravel. Carved from ivory in Benin c. 1600

For the Turks merchandise with this king, who, every year, sends him many loaded vessels to Mecca . . .
The Jesuit Priest, Peres, writing of his fear of an Ottoman
supported attack on Portuguese Malacca by the Sultanate of Aceh, 1566.

In 1497 Vasco da Gama rounded the Cape of Good Hope and by 1510 the Portuguese were threatening Ottoman Indian Ocean trade. The seeds for this revolution had been set by the Italian maritime republics of the Crusades period with their employment of portolan charts, their dedication to all-year sailing and their rapid shipbuilding technologies.

In Europe Suleiman I, the Magnificent, seemed to be having it all his own way. After the Battle of Mohacs in 1526 Hungary effectively ceased to exist, and whilst the first Ottoman siege of Vienna failed due to overextended supply lines, the writing seemed to be on the wall for the Habsburgs.

The problem for the Ottomans was that the Habsburgs were fast acquiring a global empire. The divine mission of foot soldiers and knights to Crusade and conquer in the name of Christ was being taken up by conquistadores and buccaneers. The penultimate Mamluk sultan, Al-Ghawri, fortified Jeddah with a regiment of arquebusiers and sent a rapidly-built fleet into the Indian Ocean, but after some initial success he had to seek assistance from his enemy the Ottomans as the Portuguese effected an economic war on both sultanates' trade revenues.

With Sultan Selim I's conquest of the Mamluk Sultanate in 1517 the Ottomans inherited the war with the Portuguese, which now extended into the Persian Gulf. The Ottoman admiral, Piri Reis, tried

to draw his master's attention to the risk to the entire empire from the Europeans sailing in the Indian Ocean and he produced an analysis of Portuguese activity in a prologue to his *Kitab-i-Barhriyye*, a seafaring manual. Suleiman initially showed some interest, but the opportunity to stop the Europeans at this early juncture was lost when the arms and ships built up for a campaign in the Indian Ocean were used instead in the Mediterranean in 1531.

More 'provincial' naval affairs were seen in the failure of the Ottoman siege of Malta in 1565 and the Battle of Lepanto in 1571. These were morale-boosting successes for the Europeans, but the 'Battle of the Three Kings' in 1578, which probably has the right to be called the last true Crusade, led by King Sebastian of Portugal, ended in disaster in Morocco, and events beyond the Mediterranean were to have far more impact than any of these campaigns.

The Spanish had been drawn to America for gold but also found silver. In 1540 Peru's Silver Mountain produced 148kg a year, by 1590 it was producing 3,000,000kg a year. Nothing on this scale economically had ever occurred before, or since. The resulting massive devaluation in the value of silver across Europe had a disastrous effect on the Ottoman economy, as it was based on silver coin. There were Janissary mutinies and Anatolian revolts as hyperinflation and depreciation of the currency took hold.

The Mongols also re-enter our story at this point as the Yuan Dynasty's collapse, and the Ming Dynasty's wish to isolate China from the world despite inheriting a vast navy from their predecessors, formed a vacuum in the South China Seas which allowed the Portuguese, Dutch and English to create a new world trade system. The new Crusaders were going global.

99 Troops of the British Indian Empire. Cavalry on the Tigris and Infantry in Jerusalem, 1917. Their British commanders are also seen here mixing with fellow Italian and French officers to listen to a Franciscan monk preaching

De toutes choses ne m'est demeuré que l'honneur et la vie qui est sauve ..
'All that is left is honour ...' King François I of France writing to his mother, after his defeat and capture at the Battle of Pavia, 1525. His opponent, Charles V, as a monarch of the early modern era, had moved very far from the world of the medieval knight-errant.

Charles V was no romantic, and whilst the Holy Roman Emperor burned with the fury of a zealot equal to that of any Crusader, he was also a supreme politician and was certainly no believer in the old ways of warfare. His final defeat of Francis I, the avatar of chivalry, in Italy was undertaken through a war of attrition that employed full-time professional troops and mercenaries. This would also be the key to his frustration of the ambitions of Suleiman on the eastern front. In 1527 Croatia accepted Austrian-Habsburg rule, in truth there was very little choice available to the Croatians, and the troops of the Croatian lords were assimilated into the Habsburgs' *Militargrenze* or military frontier. The *Militargrenze* at this point meant nothing more than a collection of strongholds and minor forts

manned by paid-for border troops, the core of which was the standing army that the Habsburgs had formed after their humiliation by at Domažlice in 1431 by Prokop the Bald during the fifth Crusade against the Hussites. The *Militargrenze* overlooked the main Ottoman invasion routes into Central Europe and its troops continued the fight against the Ottomans for entire campaigning seasons and beyond with raids and probing patrols.

Land warfare was becoming the domain of the foot-slogger and of entrenched musketry. The long seventeenth century opened with a nine-year Habsburg-Ottoman war, the torture of Germany by the Thirty Years War, of which the Ottomans could take very little real advantage due to the stolid Habsburg border defences, and the failure of the second Ottoman siege of Vienna.

At the century's end we see the Ottomans losing Hungary, and the debacles of the second Battle of Mohacs and Senta, as well as the rise of Russia at the Turks' expense. By the time of the Treaty of Karlovitz in 1699 the Ottoman Empire was a second-rate power, defeated not by dashing knights but by trade strangulation, stagnant technology and worldview, harem politics and accidental economic warfare.

There was also a psychological 'turning in' and avoidance of change related to the militarisation of Turkish society, a malady from which the Mamluks had also suffered. Furthermore the Crusades and the Mongol invasions had left deep scars on the Muslims of the Middle East, and caused them to destroy the Syrian coastline and to fall behind in the naval arms race that was eventually going to decide the contest with the Europeans. An idea of this pervasive dread of a repeat of events is held in the fourteenth-century Arabic myth that each new king of Cyprus would slip across to the ruins of Acre during a moonless night to have their coronation take place in the Crusader capital.

The Europeans seized their moment to look beyond the local theatre of war with their neighbours, and the invading armies of Napoleon in 1798 effectively brought modernity to the Middle East, though unfortunately in the form of massed regiments of infantry with rapid-fire musketry, mobile artillery and organised supply chains. That the Holy Land fell once again to Europeans in 1917 is not then surprising. That it fell to Europeans with Asian empires was arguably the result of a Crusading ethos.

Nazi Propaganda. Saint George draped in swastikas killing the dragon from a book about 'heraldry', and a Nazi Crusader Knight standing against the unholy faith of Bolshevism

Great was the increase, and rapid the progress, during the two hundred years of the Crusades; and some
  philosophers have applauded the propitious influence of these holy wars, which
appear to me to have checked rather than forwarded the maturity of Europe. The lives and
labours of millions, which were buried in the East, would have been more profitably employed
in the improvement of their native country: the accumulated stock of industry and wealth would
have overflowed in navigation and trade; and the Latins would have been enriched and
enlightened by a pure and friendly correspondence with the climates of the East.

Edward Gibbon's oft-quoted verdict on the Crusades.
Decline and Fall of the Roman Empire, Volume VI, Chapter LXI.

It is hard to argue against Gibbon's verdict on the Crusades, given that events such as the Children's Crusade, that are so awfully tragic and bathetic, were a creation of the Crusading phenomenon. However, I feel we perhaps need to look a little bit further than the simple action of the period and to what was occurring in the central lands of the world, and in that small peninsula of Asia called Europe

St. Georg mit dem Hakenkreuz

at this time. The Crusades were an accelerating catalyst to a society that had been 'hemmed in' by Vikings, Muslim raiders and Magyars. The challenge was created by exceptional clerics who threw down a gauntlet to thuggish kings and knights to look beyond backyard blood feuds and to new horizons. There could have been no Crusades without the Cluniac reform of the Medieval Church, and without the revival of intellectual rigour in the papacy under Gregory VII and Urban II. Much of this energy had ironically been generated by classical learning 're-entering' Europe via Spain and Sicily in the form of Arabic and Jewish scholars' translations of and expansions upon classical scientific, mathematical and astronomical treatises, but equally there could have been no

Crusades without the knightly adventurers' adamantine endurance and the Italian sailors' élan. The two components fed off each other.

What perhaps is more of an issue several centuries later is that the violence of the Crusades has commonly been divorced from its spiritual and intellectual components (though in truth they *were* not uncommonly separated at the time – chivalry could be just the tinsel to obscure the bloodiness of reality) and the word 'Crusade', like 'Jihad', has become a catch-it-all for violent actions, and ludicrous ideologies, divorced from any deeper understanding of the original motivations of these doctrines.

The Nazi Alfred Rosenberg, soon to be Reichsminister for the occupied eastern territories, on the eve of Operation Barbarossa embraced the martial element of Crusading but detached the religious element of selflessness:

Today we are not mounting a Crusade against bolshevism simply in order to free the poor Russians from this bolshevism for all time no it is in order to pursue German policy . . .

But the true Crusader and the true Mujahid were converted by their mission, and we must understand that a much more straightforward question of faith, salvation and identity was at play in the medieval age. Mediaeval communities were defined by religion, and religion demarcated identity. Salvation through allegiance was always to be sought, and Crusading and Jihad both offered it. As Urban II stated:

Let those who have been robbers now be soldiers of Christ, let those who have been hirelings for a few pieces of silver now attain an eternal reward . . .

It is a hackneyed truism that the past is a foreign country and that they do things differently there, but objects can connect us to the people of that strange land and to their passions, fears, and ambitions. They help us gain a greater understanding of these peoples' mortal faults, but also of their preternatural understanding of the eternal value of beauty and of their need to create objects worthy of reverence.

Index

Abagha, Mongol Ilkhan 186, 191–2, 194, 197

Abbasid Caliphs 15, 21, 25, 47, 98–9, 111, 128, 138, 174, 184, 194

Acre 58, 144–5, 147–51, 154, 156, 161, 172, 180, 186, 190–1, 198–201, 241

Ademar, Bishop of Puy 36, 38, 44–5, 52

Adrianople 205, 207

Ager Sainguinis, Battle of 85

Akritai 204

Al-Adil, Ayyubid Sultan 153, 155, 159, 160

Al-Afdal, Ayyubid Sultan 140, 142, 159

Al-Afdal, Wazir of Egypt 48, 56, 61, 80–1, 93

Al-Andalus 12–13, 56

Al-Ansari, military treatise writer 184–5

Albania 205, 207, 210–11, 213

Albigensian Crusade 165, 214, 217, 222

Al-Bursuqi, Governor of Mosul 88–9

Aleppo 21, 42, 64, 77–9, 82–4, 88–9, 97–8, 104–05, 109–11, 124, 128, 130, 132, 134, 138–9, 154, 159, 176, 182, 192, 210

Alexander Nevsky, Grand Prince of Kiev 218, 221

Alexius I, Byzantine Emperor 24, 36, 40, 42–3, 48, 63, 96–7, 137, 163

Alexius II, Byzantine Emperor 137

Alfonso X, King of Castile 222–3

Al-Hakim, Fatimid Caliph 15, 24

Al-Kamil, Ayyubid Sultan 160–2

Al-Mansura 170–1, 174, 182

Al-Tarsusi, military treatise writer 56

Amalric, King of Jerusalem 117–19, 121–4, 126, 130, 151

Anatolia 16, 18, 36, 41, 58, 63–4, 97, 100, 107–08, 117, 137, 139, 149, 169, 172, 176, 192, 204–05, 207, 213, 233, 240

Ankara, Battle of 210

Antioch 21, 24, 29–30, 38, 40–5, 49, 51–2, 54, 58, 60, 78–9, 83–5, 87, 89, 95, 97, 99, 103, 109, 112, 117, 121, 139–40, 165, 176, 184, 186, 189

Archery 16–17, 19, 29, 31, 37, 41, 50, 56, 60, 62–3, 88, 92, 110, 123, 142, 151, 154, 180, 183, 193, 208

Arghun, Mongol Ilkhan 196

Ariq Boke, Mongol contender for the Khanate 178

Armenia 39, 41–3, 87, 97, 103, 121, 176, 182, 184, 205

Arsuf, Fortress 61, 151, 152, 185

Arsuf, Battle of 151

Ascalon 51, 55–6, 79, 81, 92, 105, 115–16, 134, 144, 150–1, 154

Ascalon, Battle of 56

Askari 60, 85, 95, 98, 105

Ayn Jalut, Battle of 181–3

Ayyubid Dynasty 99, 111, 128, 130, 134, 159, 172–3, 176, 180–1, 194–5, 200

Baalbek 103

Baghdad 15, 19, 22, 72, 76, 78–9, 82, 84, 89, 97, 100, 132, 171, 174, 176, 210

Balak, Emir of Aleppo 87–8, 90, 95

Baldwin I, King of Jerusalem 39, 40, 52, 54, 58, 60, 61, 78, 81

Baldwin, Count of Edessa (II), King of Jerusalem 60, 71, 87–90, 95, 99

Baldwin III, King of Jerusalem 100, 103, 105, 111, 112, 115, 117

Baldwin IV, King of Jerusalem 130, 134, 136, 139

Balian of Ibelin, Crusader Lord 144

Ballista 35

Barbarossa, Holy Roman Emperor 149

Baybars, Mamluk Sultan 39, 69, 170–1, 176–8, 180–2, 184–6, 188, 190–4, 196, 197–8

Bayezid I, Ottoman Sultan 207–08, 210

Bayezid II, Ottoman Sultan 238

Beaufort, Fortress 186

Bedouin 47, 88, 134, 136, 180

Beirut 58, 138, 144, 159, 202

Belgrade, Siege of 238

Berke, Khan of the Golden Horde 178

Bernard of Clairvaux 33, 108

Bethlehem 54, 58, 162

Black Death 205, 223

Bogomils 214–15

Bohemond of Taranto, Crusader Lord 23–4, 26, 29, 30, 38–40, 42–4, 49, 58, 97, 107, 163, 189

Bohemond II, Prince of Antioch 60, 89, 99

Bohemond III, Prince of Antioch 121, 139

Bohemond VI, Prince of Antioch 176, 184, 186, 188

Bohemond VII, Prince of Tripoli 198

Bosnia 210, 214, 215

Bulgaria 204–05, 207–08, 210, 214

Buri, Emir of Damascus 95, 97–8

Byzantine Empire 16–18, 23–5, 35–6, 42, 44, 57, 64–5, 71, 96–7, 100, 102, 108–09, 112, 117, 121, 126, 128, 137, 150, 160, 163, 169, 190, 204–05, 208, 210, 228, 233

Caesarea 58, 151, 185

Caffa 227

Cairo 15, 80, 118–19, 122–3, 128, 138, 160, 170, 172, 176–7, 180, 183–6, 190, 198

Cannon 211, 227, 233, 242

Cavalry charge 28–31, 44, 56, 60–1, 78, 85, 88, 92, 95, 111, 122–3, 132, 141–2, 147, 151–2, 154, 170, 173, 181–3, 193, 197, 208, 211, 221, 224, 233

Central Asia 19, 112, 124

Charlemagne 25–6, 58

Charles Martel 12–13

Charles of Anjou, King of Sicily 190, 204

Charles V, Holy Roman Emperor 240

Chastellet, Fortress 136

Children's Crusade 244

China 19, 112, 178, 196, 210, 240

Chinggis Khan, Mongol Khan 171, 173, 204, 210

Chivalry 51, 75, 88, 91, 106, 132, 144, 211–12, 233, 240, 245

Christendom 24, 52, 58, 71, 100, 165, 208, 211, 238

Church of the Holy Sepulchre 15, 24, 26, 49, 52, 54, 72, 106, 112, 165, 170, 172

Coinage 135–6, 240

Conrad III Hohenstaufen, Holy Roman Emperor 106–09, 111

Conrad of Montferrat, Crusader Lord 144, 147, 153–5

Constantinople 16, 18, 23–5, 34, 109, 128, 137, 160, 163–6, 169, 190, 205, 207–08, 210, 211, 223–4, 227, 233, 238

Crak De Chevaliers, Fortress 65–6, 69, 190

Croatia 240

Crossbows 35, 56, 110, 152, 154, 170, 185, 224, 226

Cyprus 57, 150, 155, 159, 198, 201, 241

Daimbert, Archbishop of Pisa 50, 54, 58

Damascus 21, 30, 48, 64, 69, 76–90, 94–5, 97–100, 103–05, 109–10, 115–17, 119, 124, 130, 132, 143, 147, 149, 154, 156, 158–60, 171–3, 176, 182, 194–5, 197, 200–01

Damietta 126, 128, 160, 170–1

Danishmend, Emir of western Anatolia 58

Diwan al-Ustal, Department of the Navy 57

Dorylaeum, First Battle of 38

Dorylaeum, Second Battle of 107–08

Douane, Customs 115–16

Duqaq, Prince of Damascus 30

Edessa 39–40, 42–3, 52, 54, 58, 60, 78–9, 87–8,
    95, 97, 102–04, 106
Edward, Prince of England 191
Estonia 219
Ethiopians 55

Faris 38, 184
Fatimid Caliphate 14–16, 18, 72
Feudalism, Fiefs 27, 54, 58, 165, 169, 214, 218
Field of Blood, *see Ager Sainguinis*
Finland 219
Francis I, King of France 240
Frederick II Barbarossa, Holy Roman Emperor
    160–2
Fulcher of Chartres, Chronicler 29, 46, 55,
    60, 80
Furusiyya 184, 192
Futuwwa 171

Genoa 49, 57–8, 75, 91, 155, 183–4, 198,
    213, 227–8
Gesta Francorum, anonymous chronicle 26, 31,
    35, 36, 52
Ghazi 39, 100, 202
Ghuzz Turks 20, 112, 115
Gibbon, Edward 12, 244
Godfrey of Bouillon, *Advocatus Sancti Sepulchri*
    25, 38, 40, 50–2, 54–5, 58
Grand hunts 17, 38, 124
Great Schism 24, 167, 227
Greek Fire 96, 185
Gregory VII, Pope 27, 244
Gunpowder 211–12, 226, 227, 233
Guy of Lusignan, King of Jerusalem 69, 139–45,
    147, 154–5

Habsburg Dynasty 238, 240–1
Hagia Sophia 23, 25, 227
Haifa 58
Hama 75, 95, 98, 132, 182, 190, 193
Harbiyya, Battle of 170, 172, 174

Harim 121
Hattin, Battle of 69–70, 141–3, 156
Hazagand 31
Henry of Champagne, King of Jerusalem 149,
    155, 161
Holy Lance 144
Homs 46, 82, 100, 172–3, 190
Homs, Battle of 197–8
Horns of Hama, Battle of 132
Horse archers 16, 17
Hospitallers, Military Order (*see also* Saint John)
    69, 71–2, 73, 140, 143, 155, 190, 198, 201,
    208, 221
Hugh of Vermandois, Crusader Lord 27
Hulegu, Mongol Ilkhan 171, 174, 176, 178, 182,
    184, 186, 194
Humphrey of Toron, Crusader Lord 70,
    123, 136
Hungary 205, 207, 210, 213, 238
Hunyadi, Jonas 211, 213–14, 233, 238
Hus, Jan 224
Hussites 224–6, 241

Ibn al-Athir, chronicler 22, 44, 46, 51, 88, 102
Ibn al-Khashab, *Qadi* of Aleppo 82, 85, 88–9
Ibn Al-Qalanasi, chronicler 18, 76, 84–5, 95, 97,
    105, 115
Il-Ghazi, Emir of Mardin 78, 83, 84–5, 87,
    88, 95
Inab, Battle of 110–11
Infantry 12, 15, 29, 30, 38, 44, 55–6, 60, 61, 63,
    92, 95, 105, 110, 116, 122, 132, 141, 147–8,
    150–1, 154, 160, 170, 183, 188, 201, 208,
    211–14, 218, 224, 227–8, 233, 240, 242
Innocent III, Pope 160, 218, 221–2, 227

Jaffa 48–9, 58, 60–1, 78, 92, 134, 144, 151–6,
    162, 186
James I, King of Aragon 222
Janissaries 207–08, 210, 213–14, 228,
    238, 240

Jeddah 69, 137–8, 238

Jerusalem, city and Kingdom of 14, 22, 24–8, 33, 35, 38–40, 45–9, 51–2, 54–5, 58, 60, 63, 69–72, 75, 78–9, 95, 97, 99, 106, 108–19, 116–17, 123, 130, 132, 137, 139–40, 144, 149, 151, 153–5, 158, 160–3, 165, 167, 171–2, 185, 208, 213, 218, 221, 228, 231, 233, 240

Jews 15, 34, 51, 81, 116, 244

Jin Dynasty 112

John II, Byzantine Emperor 97, 100, 102

John of Capistrano, Bishop 238

Joscelin, Count of Edessa 87, 88

Joscelin II, Count of Edessa 103–04, 112

Joscelin of Tel-Bashir, Crusader Lord 77

Karak, Fortress 69–70, 126, 138

Kerbogha, Emir of Mosul 42–4

Khila, Robe of Honour 80

Khitans 112, 115

Khurasan 18–19, 36, 103

Khwarazmians 172, 173, 180, 195

Kilij Arslan, Sultan of Rûm 31, 38, 63, 65, 117, 139, 172

Kit Buqa, Mongol General 179–81

Kosovo, First Battle of 205, 207

Kosovo, Second Battle of 233

Kurds 99, 111, 128, 132, 141, 150, 154, 176, 180, 205

Kutná Hora 224

Ladislaus III, King of Poland and Hungary 213–14

Las Navas de Tolosa, Battle of 222

Lazar, Prince of Serbia 207

Lepanto, Battle of 240

Livonia, Crusade of 218

Louis I, King of Hungary 205

Louis VII, King of France 106, 109, 111

Louis IX, King of France 170–1, 186, 190, 198

Maarrat al-Numan 45–7, 84, 100

Macedonia 205

Magyars 13, 244

Mail, chain 31, 63, 132, 134

Malikshah, Saljuq Sultan 20–2, 65

Malta, Siege of 240

Mamluk Sultanate 75, 85, 171, 180, 184, 194, 196, 210, 238

Mangonel 35, 51, 69–70, 100, 110, 150, 185–6, 199, 200–02

Manzikert, Battle of 16–18

Marinids, Sultans of Morocco 222

Marj al-Suffar, Battle of 88

Marj Ayyun, Battle of 136

Mecca 69, 126, 138, 144, 190, 238

Mediterranean 49, 56–8, 69, 96, 136, 149, 163, 165, 178, 233, 240

Mehemmed II, Ottoman Sultan 227–8, 238

Melisende, Queen of Jerusalem 100, 103

Mercenaries 17, 105, 116, 140, 204, 213, 240

Militargrenze 240–1

Milites Sancti Petri 27, 38

Minbar 76, 171

Ming Dynasty 240

Mohacs, First Battle of 238

Mohacs, Second Battle of 241

Mongke, Mongol Khan 174, 178

Mont Gisard 134, 140, 156

Mosul 15, 42, 77, 88–9, 97, 98, 104, 111, 124, 128, 132, 139, 154, 160, 176

Murad I, Ottoman Sultan 205, 207

Murad II, Ottoman Sultan 211–14

Myriokephalon, Battle of 137, 169

Naft, Naptha 110, 145, 170–1

Napoleon 242

Nazareth 144, 181, 185

Nestorian Christians 112, 185

Nicaea 35, 37, 63, 96, 108

Nicopolis, Crusade of 208, 210

Nizam al-Mulk, Saljuq minister 20

Nizari Ismaili Assassins 20, 65–6, 72, 76–7, 81–2, 88–9, 91, 93, 95, 97–8, 130, 132, 134, 154, 155, 173–4, 191
Normans 23–4, 27, 29, 42–4, 50–1, 54, 57–8, 80, 97, 112, 145, 160, 163, 189
Nur al-Din, Sultan of Syria and Egypt 39, 94, 104–05, 109, 111–12, 115–19, 121, 123, 124, 126, 128, 130, 139, 156

Order of the Dragon 210, 211, 215
Orhan, Ottoman Sultan 205

Papacy 14, 27, 58, 208, 2113, 218, 221–2, 244
Pavia, Battle of 240
Persian Gulf 128, 238
Philip II, King of France 150, 154
Pisa 48–9, 54, 58, 75, 90, 91
Polo 124
Portugal, Portuguese 12, 112, 222, 238, 240
Prague 33–4, 205, 224
Prester John 112, 115, 171, 193
Prussia 165, 219, 221

Qalavun, Mamluk Sultan 196–9
Qatwan Steppe, Battle of 19, 115
Qutuz, Mamluk Sultan 177–8, 180–2, 184

Ramla 48, 60–1, 81, 93, 134, 156
Raymond of Antioch 97, 103, 104, 109, 111
Raymond of Saint Gilles and Toulouse 38, 42, 45, 47, 50, 51
Raymond II of Tripoli, Crusader Lord 100
Raymond III of Tripoli, Crusader Lord 139–40, 142
Reconquista 13, 27, 106, 217, 221–2
Red Sea 15, 69, 119, 128, 138
Relics 166–9, 190
Reynald of Châtillon, Crusader Lord 69, 138, 140, 143, 144
Ribats 71
Richard I, King of England 150–6

Ridwan, Prince of Aleppo 77, 82–3, 98
Robert Guiscard, Norman Lord 24, 97
Robert of Normandy, Crusader Lord 54
Roger, Prince of Antioch 78–9, 83–5
Roger II, King of Sicily 80, 163
Romanus Diogenes, Byzantine Emperor 16–17
Rome 27, 35, 58, 165, 208, 222–3

Saint Lazarus, Military Order of 75
Saint John, Military Order of (see also Hospitallers) 75
Saint Symeon 42, 109, 185–6
Saladin, Sultan of Syria and Egypt 32, 39, 56–7, 70, 75, 94, 118–19, 121, 123–4, 126, 128, 130–2, 134–59, 161, 184, 185, 194, 200
Saljuq Sultanate 15–22, 26, 39, 41, 72, 77, 87, 89, 112, 115, 172
Sanjar, Saljuq Sultan 18–19, 115
Sapping 103, 150, 185, 191, 201, 227
Serbia 204–05, 207–08, 210, 213, 233, 238
Shahid 39, 98, 104
Shirkuh, Ayyubid Lord 111, 119, 121–3, 130, 136
Sigismund, Holy Roman Emperor 224
Sigismund, King of Hungary 208, 210
Sinan, Nizar Ismaili Assassins Master 130, 132, 134, 155
Skanderbeg, Albanian Lord 211, 213, 238
Smyrna 205
Stephen, Prince of Moldova 238
Suleiman I, Ottoman Sultan 238

Tal Danith, Battle of 79
Tancred of Hauteville, Crusader Lord 39–41, 44, 50–1, 58, 87, 97
Tarsus 39, 56, 97
Templars, Military Order 71–2, 75, 95, 140–1, 143, 147, 151, 155, 170, 185–6, 189–90, 201
Teutonic Knights, Military Order 75, 180, 218, 221
The Three Kings, Battle of 240
Thirty Years War 241

Tiberias 78, 140–2, 144

Tikrit 99

Timur Leng, Turkish Warlord 210

True Cross 54, 141–2, 150, 153, 160

Tughtigin, Emir of Damascus 77, 79–80, 95, 100

Turcomen 16, 17, 31–2, 38, 41, 60, 85, 95, 102–03, 107, 110, 139–40, 180, 184

Turcopoles 116

Tutush, Emir of Syria 21–2

Tyre 49, 58, 69, 71, 79, 87, 89–90, 92, 103, 110, 144–5, 147, 149–50, 202

Urban II, Pope 14–15, 17, 24, 26–8, 33, 51, 72, 244–5

Usama Ibn-Munqidh, chronicler and warrior 31, 79, 137

Varna, Crusade of 212–13

Vasco da Gama 238

Vassalage 33, 52, 58, 78, 97, 111, 207–08, 210, 233, 238

Venice 15, 25, 49, 57, 75, 87, 89–91, 159, 163, 166, 169, 190, 198, 205, 213, 227–8

Vienna 238, 241

Vikings 13, 165, 241

Vlad Dracula, Prince of Wallachia 238

Wallachia 208, 210–11

War wagons 211–12, 214, 226, 233

William of Tyre, Chronicler 71, 92, 103, 110

Zangi, Emir of Mosul 39, 98–100, 102–05, 111

Žižka, Jan, Hussite warlord 224–6